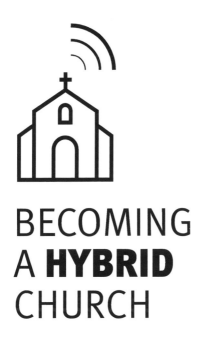

BECOMING
A **HYBRID**
CHURCH

Dave Daubert and
Richard E. T. Jorgensen, Jr

All biblical quotes are from the World English Bible, a public domain mod-ern translation based on the American Standard Version.

Larger quantities of this book are available at a discount. For information on purchasing for orders larger than 10 copies, contact the publisher at Resources@Day8Strategies.com

ISBN: 978-0-9910621-2-6

Day 8 Strategies

1132 Morningside Dr.
Elgin, IL 60123

To contact the authors send an email to: Resources@Day8Strategies.com

Table of Contents

How to Use This Book

A book like this is a chance to look at how you are currently doing ministry in the congregational setting where you live and work. The pandemic changed the world – not just for a little while but in ways that will impact the church for the next chapter of our work. With all of the challenges that have been thrust upon us by contextual changes, each of us is now being called to think about how to respond to and even proactively engage in the hard work of discovering a new future.

This book is written to help you do that work. The "you" in that sentence could be singular – you the reader reading and reflecting. But ideally the "you" in that sentence is plural – you working together as a group or even team of people. The best thinking about a future that is rapidly coming to us is rarely done alone. Each of us brings insights, questions and ideas to the table. Each of us bring blind spots and gaps as well. That's why this book is written with a way for you to reflect, perhaps alone, but even more so, perhaps with others.

If you are using this book with a small group, a staff, a leadership team or your congregation's board, taking the book one or two chapters at a time will work well for you.

The book is written with chapters written to be easily read in a single sitting. Most people will not need more than 20-30 minutes to read chapters of this length. Choose the pace that works for you and the people you are reading with.

At the end of each chapter is a set of materials for you to use. Of course, you can read and reflect using these alone, if you are reading the book by yourself. But the goal of these sections at the end of each chapter is to provide a simple framework to reflect on and discuss the content of the chapter you just read.

If using this book with a group, here are simple instructions for the work:

- Decide when and where you will meet

- Be clear who is going to lead the discussion – easy to do since the questions are provided for you!

- Assign the chapter(s) that you will discuss and ask everyone to read the material prior to the meeting. Ask them to also be sure look at the questions and ideas for reflection. Sometimes there may be a suggestion to do a little online searching before attending the group.

- At the discussion session:

  ‣ Be sure everyone knows everyone

  ‣ Read and discuss the scripture passage to open the formal time

  ‣ Work through the questions. There are three kinds of questions: share, reflect and act. Each contains one or more questions to help you think about the content of the chapter and how it connects to your life and the work of the church in your setting.

- ▶ Close with prayer. There is a prayer to end each chapter's discussion, but we encourage you to also take time to share prayer concerns that are personally important to the participants as well.

- ▶ Be clear when the next session will take place, where it will meet, who will lead the discussion next time, and which chapter(s) you will discuss.

This kind of format it easy – you can do it. And it builds the chance for new insights, shared learning and the ownership of ideas that can help you not only think about this, but also actually begin to move forward!

Introduction

If anyone had predicted on Ash Wednesday 2020 that by Easter Sunday almost every church building would be closed, we would not have believed them. But that is exactly what happened. By mid-March 2020, we were confronted by a pandemic and all over the United States and the world, people were observing "stay at home" orders. Restaurants, movie theaters, fitness centers and countless other businesses and institutions were closed. And our church buildings were closed too, but that does not mean that we were closed. Rather, it was a time for us to learn new ways of being the church.

The timing of all of this resulted in news stories all over the country focused on what churches were going to do now that they were "closed for Easter." But God's church never closed – just moved – and many congregations had found ways to offer worship online. Not surprisingly, there were many people who were curious to see what we were doing. As a result, we had an unprecedented number of people who worshipped with us and heard the Good News of Jesus' death and resurrection.

One of the encouraging discoveries from that time was learning that we were capable of doing things we might have never imagined even two months earlier. It was a good reminder that we often learn new things out of necessity. In some ways, being challenged had some hidden blessings. But in the weeks and months that followed we also learned that there is a significant difference between responding to a crisis and actually living into a new reality.

We wrote this book because we believe that God is calling us to become a new kind of church to live into a new kind of future. Among the most obvious changes we face in moving forward is that our on-the-ground gatherings will look different. And having discovered our potential for online ministry, and connecting with new people, we certainly don't want to forget what we've learned, nor neglect this opportunity to serve God and neighbor in ever expanding relationships not just in our neighborhoods but often throughout the country and around the world.

In short, we believe that God is calling us to discover our future as a **hybrid church** that embraces both online and on-the-ground ministry as equally important for our future. If we ignore either of these, we do so at our own peril.

Our online mission is more than an add-on to our on-the-ground ministry. It is a mission field. While we can interact with people who physically participate in various ministries on-the-ground, we have the potential to interact with virtually anyone (that was a pun) in the world online. Almost 100 percent of people we are trying to connect with spend time online – some of them a lot! And we don't have to wait for them – we can go to them online – meeting them in their homes, workplaces, and many other places where they are as they also spend time in the digital world.

That means that online ministry is not really "virtual" at all – we are connecting with real people in real time. What has changed is that we are learning how to connect with people using technology we may have neglected before. Whether we are connecting with people in our buildings or online, we have the same call to connect with people in deeper ways that invite people to move from being more than an audience in worship to full participants in the Gospel of Jesus Christ. And whether we are connecting with people in our online or on-the-ground settings, we are invited to discover new possibilities we may not have imagined before, and to also remember our call to make disciples of Jesus in whatever setting we are called to serve.

The purpose of this book is to help you and your congregation begin to discover your path forward. It is our hope that this book will be used by leadership teams, church boards, councils, and small groups as a catalyst for faithful conversations. We also hope that you will read this as a call to renewed action as you engage your community both online and on-the-ground in ministry and mission which really matters to God.

In the chapters which follow, you will find reflections on different aspects of ministry in the hybrid church. We also include Biblical texts with each chapter which we hope will ground your conversations in listening to God and one another. There are also discussion questions for further reflection, and we encourage you to create your own questions as well. Some of what we present may seem familiar, and other things may seem new or challenging, and we invite you to receive all of this with an openness to what God might be dreaming for you.

We do not write as experts (not even close!) on this new reality, but as fellow leaders and learners. We believe that we are all partners in the Gospel, and we trust that God has already given you the gifts and resources to live into the future. We want to be a part of a larger learning community which embraces our call to participate in God's work, wherever God may lead us. We will make missteps and discover that some days there are no perfect answers. Moving forward, the more space we allow one another to be creative, to learn, to engage and sometimes to fail, the more we will be able to do our best work as we continue the ministry of Jesus.

As you read this book, we pray that God who has already begun a good work among you will continue to guide and bless you as you live and grow into God's future, on-the-ground and online.

Dave Daubert and Richard E. T. Jorgensen, Jr.

1

The Hybrid Church and Adaptive Leadership

The church learned an incredible amount in a very short time when the COVID-19 crisis hit during early 2020.

Had anyone on February 15th of that year suggested cancelling all in-person Easter worship as a strategic move in order to make resources available for an online outreach strategy, they would have been received with shock and strong opposition. But less than two months later, a significant majority of congregations had cancelled in-person worship and moved to online, often with good and surprising results. Various sources have noted that the broad social connections caused by a shared pandemic, high media attention to Easter being online, and the fact that congregations were able to pull this off meant that Easter 2020 may have been the most impactful Easter since the first one when Jesus' followers found the empty tomb – all because the church had no choice but to adapt or disappear.

That's an important lesson about adaptive leadership. It is easier to adapt when you have no choice except to do it. This is because our instincts often encourage us to maintain current norms, traditions and practices and then simply modify them from time-to-time – a tweaking approach to leading. But when a crisis comes, people are more likely to clearly see the things that are killing or hurting them and more open to try new things that promise the possibility of life. In other words, while not everyone is wired the same and responds with equal creativity, all of us can be more adaptive based on circumstances and motivation. This is a hopeful reality.

Becoming a *hybrid congregation* requires a significant amount of adaptive leadership and an equal amount of adaptability from the entire organization. That's because taking online ministry seriously in ways that use it in its fullest, most effective forms will not only add an online presence to the congregation, it will also change its on-the-ground ministry. Being a hybrid congregation does not mean that you just add online ministry and keep the other things the same; being a hybrid church means rethinking and reforming *all* of the ministry of the congregation. That's what makes being a hybrid church challenging – rethinking everything is a big task. But that's also what makes being a hybrid church exciting – rethinking everything opens new doors for the entire ministry of the church!

So what is adaptive leadership and how does it shape the kinds of work that a congregation needs to engage in in order to become a hybrid ministry?

On the one hand, adaptive leadership is nothing new. You can look throughout history and where challenges have been met and amazing new things have happened, the use of adaptive leadership skills is in full view. The ability to adapt, innovate and move forward is a hallmark of creative movements in every aspect of human life. It has been the stuff of history when difficult challenges have not only been met but also paved the way for a completely new future.

The term and concept of adaptive leadership is actually relatively new. Martin Linsky, Ronald Heifetz and Alexander Grashow coined the terms "adaptive" and "technical" leadership in work that is only about a decade old (*The Practice of Adaptive Leadership*, Harvard Business Press, 2009). Sometimes people who misunderstand these terms pit them against each other as if adaptive means "good" and technical means "inadequate." In reality, this is not the case at all.

Both adaptive and technical solutions are important. The key is having the skills to lead utilizing both and the wisdom to know which kind of challenge is being faced. Apply a technical solution to an adaptive situation and the outcome is not likely to be impressive. Apply an adaptive solution to a technical problem and the result may be chaos. But if you understand what is needed and what will produce positive, appropriate results you'll be recognized for being the wise leader that you are.

In some cases, an issue has to do with working within the current system to solve a problem or improve performance. In those situations, the key is having a person or team who understand the issue and have the insights, skills and capacity to work on it. Usually a technical issue is located inside of an overall system in a way that it serves some particular aspect of the bigger picture and fits within that picture in a clearly defined way. Technical solutions contribute to some important part of the work and its advancement, but at the same time, they rarely define the work – they fit within a framework to move the organization forward.

Other times, the work goes to the heart of a group's focus and understanding of its mission. It changes the vision and reorients the ministry. This may be a significant aspect of the ministry or it may literally reorient the entire sense of mission for the congregation. When adaptive challenges arise, the group's ability to be open to new paradigms and develop innovative and creative solutions is the key to making necessary decisions and actions to move forward.

When the COVID-19 pandemic hit, everyone was pressed to deal with adaptive situations. Had anyone on Ash Wednesday 2020 suggested that all congregations should shut down on-the-ground ministry and go only online for Easter, they would have been greeted with some real resistance – much of it probably even vitriolic. But, when the pandemic hit, almost everyone moved instantly to a point of consensus – the old way of doing Easter would not be an option this time around. This universal agreement meant that making quick and decisive moves and implementing them in a short period of time resulted in people who would have previously opposed online worship now expressing gratitude for the ability to make Easter worship happen online. Even more so, many were amazed at how they experienced Easter online, how they felt about the leaders who had made it possible and were surprised to find themselves now advocates for it. While we don't want to minimize the shift that happened and the work it took to make that move, the universal agreement that the previous model and practices weren't going to work made quick shifts in mindsets and rapid progress possible.

So, what can we learn from this? What are some key elements that help leaders move an organization through a major challenge or change?

First, the clearer the challenge is and the more clearly leaders can identify and define the issues for the larger group, the better chance there can be movement and change. In the COVID-19 situation, the move to online Easter was a simple one to point to and define. Everyone could see it; health department and government guidelines made the issue even more clear and the church simply had to deal with it or fall on its face. This crisis was almost self-defining and almost everyone could understand it. While there could be controversy about *how* to respond, there was little controversy that something significant had happened and the impact of this challenge could not be ignored without serious consequence. For most of us, denial was not an option!

Second, a group benefits from urgency about the clarity of the issue and the need to do something as a result. In most cases, had the struggle about online ministry been an innovation from some forward-thinking person, very little real progress would have happened between Ash Wednesday and Easter. The universality of the issue and the impact that everyone felt led to a general consensus that acting quickly on this was important and could not be ignored.

Third, people need to see a way forward – it is not enough to agree to do something. A vision of what that something is and how it will provide a way forward is essential. Once again, because on-the-ground, in-person ministry wasn't an option, the immediate question became clear, "How can we do ministry that's not on-the-ground?" Entering the online world was a major paradigm shift and an obvious clear path into the future. In the process, people began to see technology not just as a way of augmenting the old way of doing ministry (a technical part of an on-the-ground world view) or just an effort to appeal to a younger part of the congregation and community, but as an actual place to focus primary ministry (an adaptive shift to a whole new way of thinking).

Fourth, once an adaptive move is envisioned and a way forward takes the ministry into a new mindset and toward a new vision, technical solutions become essential again. In the previous paradigm, internet speeds and WI-FI networks that were adequate for email or occasionally watching videos were suddenly inadequate for dependable live streaming. While an occasional online session using the laptop's built-in webcam and microphone was more than adequate before, streaming is now primary and new cameras, different sound needs, media software, etc. all require changes in technology and some new skills. These are not inferior aspects of the work; they are the essential dance between the vision and paradigms of adaptation and the ability to actually make something happen that technical work provides.

One more word in this brief introduction to adaptation. The move to becoming an adaptive church in the COVID-19 crisis does not mean that congregations who navigated this all made the shift to becoming a hybrid congregation. When on-the-ground ministry takes place, most people have deep seated practice at living in the physical space. They are well versed in it and to many it feels good and familiar. Becoming a hybrid church will require systems to see both online and on-the-ground ministry as important and to focus strategically in *each* and *both* environments to find the way forward in each and both places.

This means that for many, staying online is just a cool way to strengthen the church's real ministry which is on-the-ground. They may be convinced that some online ministry is OK or even important, but it will never be as good as the "real" ministry where everyone is physically present or in a building. Some churches may even choose to minimize or abandon online ministry altogether, even though they spent time together there when it was a necessary alternative.

But for others, the move to online will represent a new adventure. On-site ministry will continue, but online ministry will not be just an accessory to be added on and customized but will represent a crucial step that changes the way every aspect of the church's work is envisioned moving forward.

It is for this second group that this book is written – the group which wants to make an adaptive shift.

How does a congregation rethink ministry and the tools and resources it has available to them in ways that might reshape everything? Are new ministries possible online that couldn't be pulled off on-site? Are on-site ministries able to be reimagined by moving them online or augmenting them by including online aspects in new ways? If worship is to be a long-term ministry online will we have a dedicated online experience, a mixed experience where the online is integrated into on-site experiences or cameras placed in on-the-ground worship to broadcast it? These are by no means an exhaustive list of questions. They are designed to be illustrative of the fact that hybrid ministry calls leaders to explore every aspect of ministry and use both online and on-the-ground solutions to do ministry well.

The future for the hybrid church will require leaders who can ask adaptive questions, foster adaptive conversations and help people envision innovative and creative solutions to the challenging present and future that lies ahead. Adaptive communities will learn to articulate visions and goals for the next chapter as they work together. Leaders will communicate that vision in accessible ways and help people see new ministries and their place(s) within it. That requires both the adaptive work of envisioning the future and the technical work of implementing it – using the existing skills and gifts of people and equipping people when the vision calls forth new skills and gifts from the people of God.

For Reflection and Discussion

Scripture: John 6:1-14

After these things, Jesus went away to the other side of the sea of Galilee, which is also called the Sea of Tiberias. A great multitude followed him, because they saw his signs which he did on those who were sick. Jesus went up into the mountain, and he sat there with his disciples. 4 Now the Passover, the feast of the Jews, was at hand. Jesus therefore lifting up his eyes, and seeing that a great multitude was coming to him, said to Philip, "Where are we to buy bread, that these may eat?" He said this to test him, for he himself knew what he would do.

Philip answered him, "Two hundred denarii[a] worth of bread is not sufficient for them, that every one of them may receive a little."

One of his disciples, Andrew, Simon Peter's brother, said to him, "There is a boy here who has five barley loaves and two fish, but what are these among so many?"

Jesus said, "Have the people sit down." Now there was much grass in that place. So the men sat down, in number about five thousand. Jesus took the loaves; and having given thanks, he distributed to the disciples, and the disciples to those who were sitting down; likewise also of the fish as much as they desired. When they were filled, he said to his disciples, "Gather up the broken pieces which are left over, that nothing be lost." So they gathered them up, and filled twelve baskets with broken pieces from the five barley loaves, which were left over by those who had eaten. When therefore the people saw the sign which

Jesus did, they said, "This is truly the prophet who comes into the world."

Questions

1. How does the mindset of Jesus differ from that of the disciples in the midst of the challenge they are facing in the text above? Which mindset is most prevalent in your congregation? Be sure to give examples to support your answers

2. When has a big shift made adaptive change necessary in your own life and what motivated you to make the change?

3. In what ways has open communication and dialog been used among your leaders and in your congregation to help inform and shape your congregation's adaptive response? In what ways might you wish to further expand communication both within and beyond your congregation?

4. Can you name a significant adaptive decision your congregation has made? What technical adjustments did you need to make this possible?

5. In what ways would more training or outside support (consulting and coaching) help you and others in the congregation walk through these big shifts? Has your congregation ever tapped outside expertise to walk through a challenging time?

6. What are some aspects of your congregation's life and ministry where you might need to practice adaptive leadership in order to move creatively into the future?

Prayer

Creative and loving God, you are constantly at work moving our world from where it is toward your dream. We thank you that, in spite of the challenges of our world, you are unstopped in your commitment to us and undaunted by the immensity of the work. We pray that your loving and persistent Spirit would inspire in us the same creativity, love and ability to change that has marked your involvement in our world from the beginning. Help us as leaders to see the big picture and adapt, to see the specific choices we need to make and act, and to share and inspire others in the church and in the world to join you as you call us forward into your future. We pray in the name of Jesus. Amen

2

Worship in the Hybrid Church

Now that the church has discovered the digital world in an urgent and significant way, it is increasingly clear that many congregations will need to move core functions to the online world. This brings with it all sorts of opportunities and challenges. Legitimately being a hybrid church for worship can be very stressful. You remember the worship wars where contemporary and traditional songs and liturgies were pitted against each other? The same kind of stress is possible around online and on-the-ground worship as well. And worship decisions are huge, since worship is the one aspect of ministry that usually involves the largest numbers of people. If someone is viewed as "active" in most settings, they likely attend physical worship. And the more regularly they attend worship, the more active they are seen to be. So what happens when people attend worship online most often or even exclusively?

Worship in the hybrid church will need to hold to some of the same core principles that worship has always had at its center. These are not unique to either a physical gathering or an online one. Worship always focuses on God at the center, grounds the faith community in the scriptural and ongoing story of God in Christ, and invites people to participate in this ongoing story while responding to the actions of God in their midst. While different traditions share a variety of practices, sacramental traditions include visible signs of God's Word and action – most often in Baptism and Communion – and in other ways depending on the worship tradition and theological commitments of the faith community. An even wider portion of the Christian spectrum include preaching, teaching and prayer as central to the practices of the faith community gathered for worship. This is not a chapter on what good worship looks like in a physical setting, it is about how a congregation can and should foster worship in a hybrid ministry with both an online presence and gathering in a physical space.

When the COVID-19 virus caused a variety of things to shut down in one form, expressions of the church responded in a number of different ways. Because Easter that year fell early in the physical shutdown period, people felt some urgency and even responsibility to figure out how to be online for Easter. Had the same thing happened for the 9th Sunday after Pentecost, there may not have been as much importance or consensus around making this work. But Easter meant we all had to try, and lo and behold, many succeeded in at least a functional way. Online worship was possible!

What did people discover? Online worship is real worship! Gathering online allowed for some sense of community, a way to participate in something that was meaningful and communal, a place for the scripture to be read and for preaching and teaching to happen, and a place where people could pray for and with others. While the majority of the people at online worship would gladly have returned to worshipping physically in the same place with others, a certain number of people actually preferred it! And that number grew over time.

Even if you have already been online for worship, the key step in becoming a hybrid worshipping congregation will not be going online for worship – you may have already done that. But to be a *hybrid* congregation, you will have to take time to talk about why online worship is now an integral and significant part of worship life. Being online when you can't gather is one thing but taking it seriously and freely giving up something you love in order to make it happen well and with impact is quite another. You will find that online meetings or small groups, because fewer people are involved, may be somewhat easier to welcome and accept. But adapting worship life and perhaps changing physical worship options, times and formats as part of an integrated strategy may be more difficult and complex. That's why this chapter comes first in these topics, immediately after adaptive leadership. Making this move is not always easy! And doing it well takes a lot of work.

Once you have established the why of both physical and online worship, then consider what the key elements are to being a hybrid church with regard to worship.

Treat each space as its own

Imagine you are throwing a surprise birthday party for a co-worker. You want to have food, gifts, activities and decorations for the party. What will you need and how will you prepare to assure that it's done well and results in a great party for all involved?

The answer depends significantly on where the party is

being held. Is the party going to be thrown at a picnic shelter in a park? Food, decorations and games may take on one form. Is it a surprise office party during an afternoon break at work? Then food, decorations and games may look very different. Is it being thrown at home with the assistance or facilitation of family members? Food, decorations and games could be done radically differently again. This is because putting together the same core functions effectively and engagingly takes on quite different forms and subtleties depending on who is attending, where the event happens and what kind of space is available.

Worship is no different. We often forget that much of what we do is impacted by our physical worship spaces. Anyone who has had a sanctuary with fixed pews for a long time and then remodeled it to use moveable chairs can tell you that just being able to rearrange the seating can change a lot about what we do during worship, how we do it, and how we influence the spirit and emotion of the experience. Most of our worship spaces were originally planned with certain worship functions in mind and were designed to be conducive to the things we intended to do there.

This will be a mental adjustment for many people, but online is a real place where people really do gather. Since attention to place is important when we do anything well, attention to the online space and what and how to do things there is essential. In fact, willingness to pay attention to online space in one way and physical space in another way may well be the single factor that most clearly separates a physical church that is just dabbling online from a truly hybrid congregation. A hybrid church does not prioritize one place as primary and the other as a substitute or collateral option; it places genuine energy and attention into each and everything it does.

This means that in many cases online worship is NOT just broadcasting the physical worship service. If it does involve streaming the physical service, it certainly can't be limited to setting up a camera, connecting the sound, letting it record from beginning to end and simply letting someone watch worship from a screen somewhere else – boring!

Content and Platforms

Assuming that you think and feel that your previous physical worship practices were already in somewhat good shape, what will a serious and intentional move to also take worship online involve? Being self-assured that your physical worship practices and experiences have always been done well and effectively may not always be a safe assumption – take the chance to go online as an opportunity to dig deeper into ALL your worship in a new way.

Remember that online worship is both its own thing and part of the whole worship life of the congregation. That means, at least in most cases, asking how online worship will be one part of the overall worship that we facilitate each week. Will we use the same lessons, sermon and prayers so that the core content is consistent across physical and online worship platforms? In many cases, but not all, the answer is yes. Just as some ministries add a Saturday service to accommodate and reach different people, adding online worship can be another access point not bound by a building, day or time. This is likely to be the most common pattern: a consistent message and lessons for the week in both physical and online experiences. But in some cases, you may decide that this is a chance to reach a completely different audience for worship or offer a new midweek service that stands alone or…. There are lots of options. So be intentional about what online worship is to do and who you hope to reach.

Next, remember that online worship is very different than on-the-ground worship in how some worship elements take place. Hymn singing may be meaningful in a physical gathering and seem obtuse in some online situations. That doesn't mean music during online worship isn't important – it's just different. Good song leadership on-the-ground is just bad karaoke online! Envision how it will look and feel for someone watching or listening. Preaching may be relational and focused on audience responses to cue the preacher on-site, but online preaching requires attention to the camera and may give the preacher no audience responses in real time. Prayers, readings, sacraments and many other things all need to be carefully thought through. The result will be that in many hybrid congregations, online worship will look quite different than on-the-ground worship – and both can be high quality and impactful regardless of the differences.

Another important choice is the platform and where to be when you go online. Social platforms like Facebook offer quick, relatively easy and effective places to stream worship and they require no online capacity – Facebook streams, records and stores the posts for you. And you can take a Facebook stream, get the embed code and also put the video on your congregation's web site or other places online. YouTube offers you the chance to have your own channel and to post your worship there and the Google empire means you are inside the largest search engine and most watched video platform on the planet. Vimeo is a smaller platform for video but focuses a bit more on features and quality – it may be a good spot for many, especially if you choose to produce recorded worship each week. Eventually, having a place for Sunday/weekend streaming and being on YouTube are both important. Your weekend stream is about forming community. YouTube is about being in the place where most people will be when they are searching to find sermons, worship and other faith related material (if you want to reach new people, ignore YouTube to your peril!)

New online social and video sites are continuously popping up, so do your homework and see where the people you are reaching "hang out" online. In addition, there are companies that specialize in live streaming worship and have their own platforms, equipment recommendations and methods.

As you can see, there are options to choose from. Choose based on what you can do well, what will be most effective, what functions and features will be helpful and what your budget can afford. Good quality is possible at almost any of these online locations, even with a relatively small budget. And always remember, a missional church will wisely stretch for a better option in most cases and not settle for the lowest cost that might sacrifice quality and effectiveness.

Live or recorded?"

Another issue is the question, "Live or recorded?" There are huge benefits to each of these options, but they aren't the same for you as leader or for the people who connect online.

A live stream of worship leaders in real time allows everyone who connects to do so at the same time. This can foster a larger sense of community. People can interact with each other by texting friends, paying attention to a comment stream, and with some platforms, even see each other. Prayers can be offered up in real time and people can see the names of those being prayed for in the comments stream. Live worship with a significant live online participant pool can make it helpful for a staff person or key volunteer to join in the interactions and actually greet people as they check in, comment back and forth with participants, and allow leadership and worshippers to have a more meaningful relationship. And, when it is over, worship is finished. When recorded worship is finished, there is still mixing, editing, posting and other things to be done with it – it requires additional labor-intensive steps that livestreaming doesn't.

But don't forget that live brings risks! In my (Dave's) congregation we have used live with great success. But we have still gone offline unexpectedly in the middle of worship twice. Once we got back up and running within less than a minute – just a buffering gap in the experience of most people online with us. But the other time our internet provider had an issue and we simply crashed. After seven or eight minutes we were still down and gave up on trying to get back up and returning live – most people had given up on us by then anyway! Fortunately, in that case we had completed the worship service through our children's sermon and the sermon – worship crashed as we began the prayers of the church and in the home stretch. Because we have a staff person online in the comment section doing communication, with texts between on-site staff and our online staff person, we could communicate with people what had happened and even tell them when we finally gave up! If you are live, be sure you have ways to communicate with folks if things go wrong. Once in a while – they will!

On the other hand, a recorded worship experience may lose some of the sense of being at the worship as it happens but can increase quality and participation. A musician can play or sing a piece of music, audio can be mixed for balance, and the musical piece put into a video editor. The preacher can preach. Prayers can be lifted up in a different place than where the sermon happens (i.e., the sermon is preached in the sanctuary but the prayers are led next to a fountain from a prayer garden in the church yard). Each portion of the worship can be set and led in a way that maximizes that part of the worship, and then edited together. Captions, song lyrics, leader names, graphics and even animation can be added more completely than is often possible live. When a final, higher quality edited version is finished it can be uploaded for participants. The advantage is that you can offer something of much higher quality and edit out mistakes. Because you can move the camera from place to place, you may be able to create more interest and need less equipment to produce it.

The edited, finished videos can be posted in ways that allow for a synchronized, publicized release time so everyone can watch together, almost the same experience as livestreaming. Then groups can still watch online in real time, comment to each other, and share worship as a group.

Neither recording or livestreaming is right or wrong. They both have advantages and should be considered contextually and with intentional consideration of the impacts. And remember, you can make a decision and live with it for a while, learn from that experience, and try a different method as a result. Nothing about this is permanent – just "on the way."

There are additional issues surrounding both live streaming and recorded worship options, but enough has been said here to get you started. Whichever way you go, pay attention to your context, your gifts and talents, staff capacity, what you can do well and the needs of your anticipated participants. It is best to be sure that whichever way you go – recorded or live – that you can do it well, week after week after week. This isn't something you can dabble in. It is in with both feet if you want to be a hybrid congregation.

Equipment and technology are obviously keys to pulling much of this off. If you have a good WI-FI signal and a laptop or smartphone, you can produce reasonable quality without adding much expense. Having said that, good lighting, paying attention to microphones and adding a better and dedicated camera can make a noticeable difference. The cheaper the camera, the more important lighting is and a great picture in HD is now pretty accessible for broadcasting without spending a fortune. Many people already have the capacity to stream in higher quality than many platforms support. It's easier to produce a great picture than it is to capture sound well. Remember, people will be amazed at your picture and production until they are turned off by poor, inconsistent audio! Invest in both video and audio as it makes sense, but when in doubt, audio is the place where an online church will find the most return on investment to be a meaningful and helpful online worship place.

Engagement

Relationally, remember that worship online is a real place where real people gather. When you meet someone online, say hello. For example, if you use Facebook where there is a comment stream, encourage its use for greeting each other, interactions during the sermon and lifting up prayers. Every person who comments, likes something or contributes has given you a contact point. Someone should go through every like, comment and prayer request in a comment stream and reply. Do you see someone you haven't met and don't know? They have posted a comment and revealed themselves. Find their profile, send them a message and thank them for worshipping online with you. Many will reply and interact as a result. Oddly, follow up and longer-term relationships are often much easier to do online than with people who don't fill out a visitor card in worship, even if we got to say hello and shook their hand! We will explore additional suggestions for the use of social media in the hybrid church in the next chapter.

These relationships are a central part of online worship. Don't think of this as putting on a TV program that people watch. Rather think of it as cultivating an environment in which people participate. To see what is happening, you often have to look behind the scenes. Learn to use the online analytical tools at your disposal. The platform you use will be able to provide its own analytical tools. For example, YouTube, Vimeo and Facebook have ways to share data about how many people are online, how long they watch, where they are from, etc. Look at those and especially watch trends even more than raw numbers each week. Are more people being engaged? Is our connection base stable, growing or in decline? Where are people coming from and how are they finding us? If you embed your worship on your web site be sure to set up Google Analytics or some other analytical tool to see what is happening and where people are coming from there as well. The goal is engaging people and these tools can all help you find out more about who is there and therefore, who you are trying to connect with.

Final Thoughts

At the same time, it is likely that many congregations simply won't have the resources to do online worship well – at least in ways that can reach new and unchurched people. The technology needed and the time and resource investment in some cases will be too big. So we want to emphasize the need for quality as you do this. If you can't do it well on your own – find ways to partner. Not every congregation in the country needs its own online worship! Clusters of congregations should consider pooling resources, sharing leadership and doing one online service together. If four congregations do a mediocre job, you will have four mediocre worship experiences with little engagement and outreach potential. But if they cooperate, share resources and can also have the things in place to do it well, they can all use the one final product to reach their members and have a face open to the world that is more effective.

Remember, being a hybrid church means taking your physical and online worship experiences equally seriously. This may – or may not – impact your Sunday schedule if you take this to heart. Perhaps you decide that live streaming on Sundays is the best online option. If so, what time? And if the best time for online interferes with the current physical worship times, what will you do to maximize the usefulness and impact of both? Are you willing to redesign the physical schedule and the online schedule in tandem to be most effective? What core values and ministry priorities will guide you in deciding? How will you discuss this with the people who may be most impacted and even stressed by the changes? Are you open to ideas and comments that may challenge your own research, thinking or presumptions about how to a hybrid church? Being a true hybrid church means deciding that online and on-site worship experiences are equally valuable and then weighing when and how to do them in a new and renewed mindset.

For Reflection and Discussion

Scripture: Matthew 2:1-12

Now when Jesus was born in Bethlehem of Judea in the days of King Herod, behold, wise men from the east came to Jerusalem, saying, "Where is he who is born King of the Jews? For we saw his star in the east, and have come to worship him." When King Herod heard it, he was troubled, and all Jerusalem with him. Gathering together all the chief priests and scribes of the people, he asked them where the Christ would be born. They said to him, "In Bethlehem of Judea, for this is written through the prophet,

'You Bethlehem, land of Judah,
    are in no way least among the princes of Judah;
for out of you shall come a governor
    who shall shepherd my people, Israel.'" (Micah 5:2)

[7]Then Herod secretly called the wise men, and learned from them exactly what time the star appeared. He sent them to Bethlehem, and said, "Go and search diligently for the young child. When you have found him, bring me word, so that I also may come and worship him."

They, having heard the king, went their way; and behold, the star, which they saw in the east, went before them until it came and stood over where the young child was. When they saw the star, they rejoiced with exceedingly great joy. They came into the house and saw the young child with Mary, his mother, and they fell down and worshiped him. Opening their treasures, they offered to him gifts: gold, frankincense, and myrrh. Being warned in a dream not to return to Herod, they went back to their own country another way.

Questions

1. In the text above, the magi came and worshipped Jesus and then went back to their home "another way." It reminds us that real worship is transformational – people should go home different than when they arrived.

   a. How do you see this happening in your congregation?

   b. Does the idea of worship being online make the ability to be transformed in worship more or less accessible in your mind? Why?

2. In what ways have you personally experienced worship in a hybrid church? Since online services are readily available, how could you do some research and see a variety of what others are doing?

3. What are some of the core values (officially or just unconsciously) which shape your congregation's current worship whether on-the-ground or online? Which, if any, of these values conflict with your ability to do both online and on-the-ground worship well?

4. What further adjustments to your congregation's worship practices – on-the-ground and/or online – might you think about implementing in the near future to enhance the vitality of worship in your setting?

Prayer

Amazing God, you are the one most worthy of worship and so we come to you with praise and thanksgiving first. We are so grateful for the world you have made, your commitment to it by coming in Jesus, and your commitment to us as you have made us to be your people. Our lives are truly pure gifts from you. Help us to worship, not as we are ought but as we are able. Mold and shape us and this congregation to be more and more able to worship through the work of your Spirit. As we think about worship when we are physically together, help us be inspired. And as we think about worship online, help us be equally committed and inspired as we explore and enhance our life of faith together, by your grace and in the name of Jesus we pray. Amen

3

Social Media in a Hybrid Church

The use of social ministry sites for an on-the-ground congregation is often limited in scope and narrow in its emphasis. This use can be heavily weighted toward advertisement, visibility and scrapbooking (posting lots of photos of events and gatherings). In some ways, having a web site and a Facebook page became the new Yellow Pages (remember those?) for the church that was "keeping up with the times." Web and social media presence were the new norms for bare bones advertising.

One consequence of this was that many sites remained static for long periods of time. A Facebook page had no fresh posts for weeks or even months; a website didn't post or remove information in a useful time frame for members and visitors. Then as Christmas Eve approached, the communications or evangelism committee would think of this as a good time to post an invitation to Christmas Eve worship or maybe even create an event page for the upcoming holiday. All too often, that invitation then became the only post until Easter approached and the cycle would repeat.

In this mindset, social media functioned a bit like taking out an ad in the local paper or mailing out a flyer but at a discounted rate since it cost a lot less than print and postage. Dabbling was essentially free, so people dabbled. Social media has to move to a whole new level – no dabbling allowed – if a congregation is to become a hybrid ministry.

Remember, in the new hybrid church, social media is not just accessible, it is powerful. In fact, whoever controls social media controls a lot about the church. If members are positive and engaged in healthy ways, online social media can be amazing. But if someone is disgruntled and wants to go rogue, social media means that conversations that would have happened in house before, might suddenly be public in ways that can be hard to deal with. So healthy congregational life is closely related to healthy social media life as well.

Social engagement online also has to become part of the routine for the church. This is essential because routines reflect culture. If social media is a seasonal or even just a weekly point of contact, it remains non-integral to the ministry. In a hybrid church, online presence shifts from a peripheral place in the life of the church to one that is central and dynamic.

Part of this is because social media is one of the primary places in a ministry where you can actually connect with people in their daily lives while they are in their homes, workplaces or even traveling. In other words, in a hybrid church the primary role of social media is to not advertise for people to come to you, but instead engage people in ways that allow you to go to them. Engagement, not presence, is the key. Nona Jones of Facebook said, "Engagement is everything... Don't benchmark your success on how many people watched you. You really need to figure out how many people are engaging with you." (Nona Jones, director of faith-based partnerships for Facebook. Interviewed on The Carey Nieuwhof Leadership Podcast, episode 351.)

This is a huge change for those of us who are used to posting info and ad style content. It requires a mindset shift from informational to relational interactions in a space where many of us have not yet been strategically relational. While many of us have skills and instincts for face-to-face interactions that have been honed with years of practice, only a few of us in church leadership may have the kind of relational skills and patterns to be effective at meeting and shepherding people online. And doing this isn't just a skill—someone has to make the time to do it and do it well without wasting too much time on distractions following all the rabbits down the rabbit holes that social media provides.

Building New Relationships

Being relational online means interacting. One-directional communication can still happen – it is OK to share information online! But the majority of interactions have to be designed to elicit a response and further a connection – they have to become multi-directional. You can't stop with information. While the hope of informational posts in the on-the-ground church was to raise visibility about something in order to have a person connect with us at an on-the-ground event like Christmas worship, a forum or a fundraising dinner, taking online relationships seriously means that the relationship will actually have a major portion of it, or perhaps all of it, lived out online.

Many of the same things we do when we meet people in

face-to-face situations are not that different online. We say hello. We welcome someone into our "space." We share a bit about ourselves and find out a bit about them.

People online need to do the same thing, but there are also some significant differences.

For example, the median Protestant congregation has worship attendance of well under 100 people in their physical worship. Even this small number may be divided in some settings between more than one worship service. This means that people routinely see well under 100 people at a time at church. A small congregation with a "traditional" and a "contemporary" worship may have a total attendance of 90 people each week with one service averaging 40 people and the other 50. No one except the pastor may routinely see more than 50 people in a typical weekend.

We may or may not be good at welcoming people on-the-ground, but we are almost guaranteed to spot them and know they are there. It is not even challenging. It is likely that in many worship settings like these *everyone* knows when a visitor is present 100 percent of the time!

But online ministry is different. We lose the physical cues that familiarity with a group of people and the physical presence of a new person may bring. Someone can watch our livestream worship and be online live with us and we may not know enough to connect with them. If they don't make themselves known in some way and share that they are present it can be hard for us to even know who they are, much less figure out how to start a relationship with them. We can see stats that reveal that there were a hundred people online with us, but the likes and comments only reveal the identities of fifty-three of them. Who made up the other half of worshippers this week?

Given this online dynamic, you will have to find out who is there – even when they show up!

Leaders leading online events like worship need to explicitly welcome guests to the livestream. They need to have specific ways to speak to them and invite responses. These responses may be answers to a question, a call to "like" something or inviting them to respond to some specific invitation that involves knowingly come out of the digital shadows. One congregation has a practice of posting the web address of an online contact card. Each week the online address is posted in a caption and a leader invites participants to go to that site and complete a card so they can "keep up with ministry and ways to be involved." A key is they also incentivize this invitation by saying each week, "For every new contact card filled out online, we will donate $5 to our local food pantry." This means that coming out of the online shadows helps someone else and may be the encouragement someone needs to make their presence known.

When someone does share their presence, someone from the congregation needs to be paying attention and interact with them. This isn't complicated or outside the reach of our skills: say hello, welcome them, share a quick bit about your faith community and invite them to share something back, perhaps in a private message using the messaging system within the platform where you met. Remember that we should always try to share something about ourselves first before asking others to share things about themselves; this encourages a sense of trust and helps develop mutual and reciprocal relationships.

A Path Forward

Next, there need to be places to move forward into. People who engage in faith benefit from a pathway that helps them begin the journey. Perhaps you have a contact list they can join or your congregation has a mobile app that you can invite them to use. Maybe you have a small group structure where you can offer them the opportunity to enter a group, connect with people and be invited to deepen that connection in the weeks ahead.

This means giving a lot of attention to an online environment that may have had only sporadic attention before. Online ministry done well simply uses technology as a vehicle – it is actually people-centered at its core. You will need to make time for this, have capable staff working with this and train up both skilled volunteers and an equipped membership so that people have multiple ways to interact, multiple doorways to enter into those interactions and have someone there to notice them, greet them and connect with them whichever door they enter in the online world.

Basic methodology cuts across all social media platforms you are using, but the specifics vary a lot in how each platform fosters connections and allows for follow up as relationships develop. Each ministry needs to equip its staff and members for the work in general recognizing that there are things that each platform can do or not do well.

Remember this important principle: for a contact to move to a relationship there has to be ongoing interaction. This means that a first interaction needs a place to go – some way to follow up and advance the conversation. Most congregations will need to think about their ministry, especially their online ministry, in new ways. If you meet someone online and are a hybrid congregation, then there need to be online next steps in that relationship. In the "old days," online was advertising to get people to cone to something physical. But not online has to include options for people to engage in next steps that are online. Education, service, relationships, small groups and more need to be available online or people we meet online will end up being told that "only physical presence really matters" by the passive reality that we haven't made the shift yet. Other chapters later in this book will help us think about those things, but they have to be developed early or there is nowhere and no way to engage new people online long-term.

Managing Multiple Platforms

In its early years, Facebook was the primary online social territory for young people. Now, about 69% of adults use it while the number of teenagers and young adults using Facebook has declined. (Pew Research Center, 2019)

Some online work is similar to on-the-ground ministry. Just as older, retired people tend to hang out in some places and younger adults hang out elsewhere in the physical world, the online world has its preferred niches as well. Listing them here would make the book misleading and instantly dated because the demographics of who uses them and how they are used is always evolving and changing. That said, Facebook, YouTube, Twitter, Instagram, TikTok and other sites all have an angle on interactions and a population that tends to gravitate there.

This means you need to think about who you are reaching and where they are hanging out. You also need to find meaningful ways to interact with people so you can participate with authenticity and not seem like a creepy stalker hoping to snare an unsuspecting person there. Take the time to do this well and avoid the temptation to trust your assumptions. Meet real people who use the platform and ask them to help you gain insights into the site, its culture (unspoken norms for behavior and interaction) and ways that people function best there. Learn what a platform can and can't do.

Most settings will eventually need to use more than one social media site. Facebook, Instagram and YouTube are major places where the largest audiences are right now. An active, effective online ministry will ignore them at their peril. But TikTok, Twitter and other sites are also powerful and have their own benefits and connections. We intentionally mention some of these thriving sites while not attempting to be exhaustive because new sites are emerging routinely and some of them can become significant players in a short period of time while existing ones slowly lose their allure or functional edge. All this is to say, don't assume an online solution is any more permanent than on-the-ground ones. Be alert. Stay open and curious. Keep learning.

A matrix of social media sites will begin to feel like managing a constantly changing spreadsheet. It can easily become overwhelming and all-consuming. So there are some additional things to be thinking about as you advance this work.

There are tools that allow a user to monitor, interact and post a number of things on a group of platforms. For example, posts can be scheduled and put on Facebook, Instagram and Twitter simultaneously or on some planned schedule.

Not everything has to happen in real time. These sites vary in effectiveness and ease of use and like all online tools, they are constantly changing, adding features and finding new competition. And social media sites want you to use their posting tools, so be careful to understand the benefits and consequences of posting on Facebook by using a non-Facebook application. It may be a good idea – but it may have some collateral drawbacks. And keep up with the policy changes. Literally in the weeks since we wrote this chapter and got ready to go to print, we are adding the sentence you are reading because Facebook changed its ways of working in this area in ways that impact this very paragraph. And by the time you read it – it may have changed again!

At the same time, using these tools will help you monitor and interact with people. You can watch things, observe trends of use and receive information when someone interacts with you making it less likely for you or your staff to miss a connection by overlooking something in the overwhelming sea of things that happen online.

Another reality is that more and more ministries are developing their own social media platforms by using phone apps. These are especially useful for keeping participants informed, connected and involved. You can use phone apps to set up ministry groups, manage and publicize programs, and send messages to the entire ministry community or to an individual through a personal, one-to-one note like a text message. Using cellphones as the base for these social ministry tools makes sense because they are always accessible, offer numerous tools and functions, and are increasingly preferred by people who use their phone as their primary device. Developing a custom phone app for your ministry is often as easy as signing up within a site and filling in some information; other apps are more complex and customized and can be developed by companies that specialize in phone apps for congregations.

Staffing Social Media

Remember that good social media work means being focused. Social media is a minefield of tangents and distractions. The church and staff should have accounts and pages for their work. In most cases these should not overlap with a personal page or online presence – the mixing of personal and professional on social media is already blurry. The staff pages and accounts should friend, follow and interact with people who they relate to as part of their church connections and work. Having a conversation online with someone on behalf of the faith community is also a clearer witness and connection to church life than using a personal page. Use social media to keep congregational life in the foreground throughout the week and to provide opportunities to pray, commiserate, celebrate and share with people as life happens. This can change the way the church relates to and cares for people when done well and with concern for the wellbeing and safety of those with whom you are interacting.

Dedicating staff time for this is important and teaching all people to use their social leverage online is essential – it's about equipping disciples. For example, if something is happening at church – whether an on-the-ground or online event – involving church members in using their personal social media presence to invite people, promote opportunities and share their experiences will extend your reach and witness far into the community. The real power in social media is not what happens through staff but through the wider networks of relationships that participants in every congregation have with people near and far. Using social media well means having staff doing good work to build and follow relationships online while encouraging and equipping others to do the same – God's people working together!

One last word. Online relationships can be a vehicle for any part of church life – this is part of the foundation of a hybrid congregation. Social media is a place for connections that impact every aspect of church life. In many ways this is the congregation's "fellowship hall" and "meeting space" online. This is key infrastructure that impacts almost every part of a hybrid church in both its online and on-the-ground ministries.

For Reflection and Discussion

Scripture: Mark 1:40-45

A leper came to him, begging him, kneeling down to him, and saying to him, "If you want to, you can make me clean."

Being moved with compassion, he stretched out his hand, and touched him, and said to him, "I want to. Be made clean." When he had said this, immediately the leprosy departed from him and he was made clean. He strictly warned him and immediately sent him out, and said to him, "See that you say nothing to anybody, but go show yourself to the priest and offer for your cleansing the things which Moses commanded, for a testimony to them."

But he went out, and began to proclaim it much, and to spread about the matter, so that Jesus could no more openly enter into a city, but was outside in desert places. People came to him from everywhere.

Questions

1. The text above shows the power of people meeting Jesus and having everything about their lives changed by that encounter. It was a story that could not be stopped.

    a. How is your life different because of the work of Jesus?

    b. Who have you told recently and what did you share?

    c. If it has been a while since you talked about it, what would help you restore that energy and enthusiasm to your own life of faith?

2. Social media is a way/place where people share information – all sorts of information. What is your personal experience and practice with social media? What platforms do you use regularly?

3. Look at your personal social media pages, and consider your most negative posts; in which ways does this reflect on your congregation's life and witness?

4. Think about how your congregation uses social media currently.

    a. In what ways does your congregation's use of social media reflect the faith and enhance the witness and ministry of your congregation?

    b. In what ways does your congregation use social media to nurture existing relationships and to cultivate new ones?

    c. How does your congregation equip your members to use social media as a tool for ministry and sharing your faith?

5. What are some practical next steps your congregation may take to equip your members and your staff to engage more effectively in social media?

Prayer

God of love, at your core you are Father, Son and Holy
Spirit – a God grounded in relationship. Help us to be as
relationally intentional as you are. As we encounter new
people in the world around us, whether face to face or
online, give us open hearts and minds that desire to meet
and connect with people in ways that introduce them to
your love in Christ and connect them to a life of faith in new
ways. At the same time, help their gifts and skills impact
us as we build mutual relationships that also change us
as we make new friends. In Jesus' name we pray. Amen

4

Spiritual Formation in the Hybrid Church

Recently, I (Richard) was facilitating an online small group Bible study. We had someone who was able to participate for the first time because they were now able to join the group from their home. It allowed them to simultaneously meet their family obligations and also fully participate in the Bible study. This person helped our group move deeper in our study and provided wonderful insight into their own life and faith. Although I had known this person for years, that night I actually got to know them in a way that would not have been possible in a traditional onsite gathering. It was an illuminating moment when I and others discovered that deep spiritual work could happen online.

Spiritual formation is an essential aspect of our life and ministry in the church. It is essential because whether we do it intentionally or not, we are practicing spiritual formation all the time. Spiritual formation grows out of our worship, teaching and preaching, and most especially through the habits of our hearts which make space for us to notice God's work among us. Like most things in life, intentionality increases the chances of moving forward and experiencing growth.

Invitation to a Journey, M. Robert Mulholland that "Spiritual formation is a process of being formed in the image of Christ for the sake of others." (Intervarsity Press, 2016, p. 16) We like this definition because it reminds us that spiritual formation is a process. It is intentional and it takes time. This understanding also reminds us that spiritual formation is not primarily about personal satisfaction or fulfillment; it is about being shaped in ways that enable our lives to reflect the life and love of Christ to the world.

A few years ago an online assessment tool called *Reveal* was developed to help leaders assess the health of their ministry. A particular interest of the survey's authors was to determine how involvement in congregational life helped people grow as disciples. Shockingly, they found that in general, congregational participation does not lead to spiritual growth. In other words, increased involvement in church life does not correlate to increased spiritual maturity. What they have learned is that a key factor in predicting the growth of people was whether they intentionally built spiritual practices into their daily lives. Congregations that taught and encouraged spiritual practices helped participants grow in spiritual formation and maturity.

The good news for us is that spiritual formation takes place best within a community of faith. Congregations that intentionally work at this can change lives in deep and lasting ways. Whether a congregation is gathering in person or online, it still has a calling and responsibility to make disciples who will bear witness to Christ in word and in deed. Being a hybrid church calls us to reexamine how we practice spiritual formation and to recognize the new opportunities and resources we have been given to live into this calling in new ways. Because spiritual formation is grounded in centuries of the

Christian faith, much of the work that is fresh is also deeply rooted in ancient practices. This basic connection between a meaningful present and well-grounded traditions can and will happen in both places – online and on-the-ground.

One way to start this is to increase the congregational culture's attention to spiritual awareness. This can be enhanced through good use of social media. One congregation has changed the administrative assistant's job description to include posting on Facebook and Instagram every Monday morning. This key task involves listening to the online sermon, finding a quote or two from the message that lifts up a key spiritual insight or idea, and posting a picture from the church (flowers, communion chalice, people, a cross, a stained glass window, organ pipes, etc.) that uses the quote as a caption. That post sets a tone that social media is not just a place to advertise programs; it is also a place where spiritual teaching and inspiration happens. Those posts are seen by members who are helped to see an important part of the message reinforced again during the week. The posts are frequently shared on the timelines of others and can provide a base for teaching and outreach to a wider audience.

The more the content online from the congregation is spiritually grounded, the more online work helps the entire ministry, whether on-the-ground or online.

The Importance of Small Groups

Because of the communal nature of so much of spiritual formation work, probably no other area of congregational life adapts more easily to the online world. Most congregations, especially mainline ones, have lacked the kinds of small group ministry and regular Bible study work that is essential to doing this well. In many settings, adult educational opportunities often reach well under a quarter of the active worshippers. Small groups, if they exist at all, include only a fraction of participants as well. Many leaders are frustrated that these areas of important work haven't gone better – but progress in many settings has been slow.

On-the-ground small groups are often difficult to sustain. People often struggle due to time commitments and schedules. The difficulty of getting people to commit to something that is 75-90 minutes long plus drive time to and from the group – add childcare and homework issues for those with kids – means many have been reluctant to join. This isn't opposition as much as reluctance – people just can't envision giving up 2-3 hours without feeling jammed up. So they don't.

But jump online and see what happens. People can be home and not need childcare and eliminate the evening commute to a group after just getting home from the evening commute from work. They can start when the session begins and be home the second it ends. Now people can see themselves making this work – groups can pop up and succeed.

Whether a congregation gathers in person or online, it is essential to cultivate a practice of helping people see all aspects of life as sacramental – that God is always present and active. The more this foundation is understood and owned, the easier it will be to help people see God as present in both online and physical settings. Remember this crucial truth: we don't need to be physically present with one another to know that we are all simultaneously in the presence of God.

This sacramental reality means that the starting point for spiritual growth is always God. Helping people be more alert to God's presence and action is essential and this means seeing life in two directions. One is "inside-out" – the practice of recognizing that everything which happens within the congregation helps us be aware of God among us and also points us out in service toward the world. The other way of seeing is "outside- in" – a pattern for spiritual formation that recognizes that Christ is also already out there in both our physical neighborhoods and in the online communities in which we participate.

Gatherings, whether on-the-ground or online, need to cultivate a sense that "God is in here." At the same time, these same gatherings need to open people up to watch, listen and join in with a God who is also "out there."

A key for leaders to help make this happen will be recruiting leaders, lifting up the importance of groups for spiritual growth and discipleship, and providing resources and support for groups to have what they need. Giving groups a simple template for a good way to frame their time can be helpful. Selecting or providing curriculum or resources can keep group quality high. And remember that an online group (or on-the-ground one as well) can share screens and watch video resources together is one step that can make the quality and engagement of small groups higher. Many people are making the case that all ministry, even on-the-ground ministry, should be "screen ready" so that something that can be watched in worship on Sunday, can be watched in a small group on Tuesday, or individually on Friday as well. Good spiritual growth resources can find their way into many levels of the church's work!

There are many ways to improve our engagement with people once you have this base to work from. Some will be online small groups. Some will be physical gatherings of small groups. Some groups may include a mix of both.

Concerning using both, I (Richard) have been gathering a group on Thursday evenings once a month to reflect on scripture and invite people to consider ways of living and proclaiming the Gospel. The online gatherings are possible whether leaders and members are at home, church or on the road and don't require anyone to go through the logistics and time required to travel back and forth to the church building.

Over time, the group developed a pattern of meeting online multiple times each month – some online and some together physically. Neither the in-person or online gathering is better than the other because they complement one another. We soon noticed that some people from the in-person group didn't participate online (and this didn't always follow stereotypes about age and technology). At the same time, we added participants who simply were unable to attend the in-person gatherings but welcomed the online opportunities. Seeing and learning from this has led to other ways to gather hybrid groups in which we have some people who gather at the church while others participate from home. In many ways, this has been the most satisfying because it allows us to accommodate the various needs and situations of each participant while maximizing the number of people who can participate.

In these initial examples, you can probably see that hybrid congregations can cultivate an even wider awareness of God's presence among us than those limited to on-the-ground teaching. Using more diverse tools and environments can help each of us remember that we are always participants in something greater than ourselves and that our ultimate hope rests in God. By expanding how people see this truth beyond their own physicality, peoples' sense that God is even bigger than they had previously imagined can be nurtured in healthy, life-giving ways.

Don't Work Alone

As church leaders, we bring a bias that the church functions best in collaborative ways – always mindful that each of us fully represent the body of Christ in our setting but never comprise the body of Christ in its fullness. The work of Jesus includes us and extends beyond us. Within this mindset, hybrid congregations function best when they see themselves as mission outposts that share a common calling and purpose with other congregations and the whole church to proclaim the Gospel and serve as Christ for the neighbor. Practicing hybrid ministry invites us to see the many ways congregations can work together for spiritual formation.

Even among congregations who have worked well together in the past, there has often been a tendency to practice many aspects of spiritual formation on their own, rather than see the potential benefits of developing deeper partnerships and opportunities with others. Using online platforms, congregations which are miles apart can now find new ways to learn and grow in faith together. This allows congregations to have an increased capacity to nurture and encourage spiritual growth through shared experiences, resources and leaders. It can make ministry more afford-able and feasible in places with limited resources. This will also open all sorts of opportunities to have access to more resources and teachers than had ever been possible before.

A wonderful example of shared learning has been seen as many congregations have discovered the benefits of part-nering together to offer shared confirmation classes online. Some teachers quickly discovered that many youth were more engaged using electronic media than when meeting physically. They observed that when they went online with confirmation, they were meeting young people on their own turf and in a space familiar to them. The practice of shared learning also allowed multiple gifted teachers and facili-tators to work with a diverse group of young people at one time. This created the opportunity for one or more people to facilitate the teaching and conversation, while another per-son interacted with the class using the chat feature. Using multiple levels of engagement expanded the ways people participated in a class and provided a learning platform that was often more effective than previous confirmation models.

In doing this kind of work with adults, one congregation's staff member began to use the online environment as a way of gathering a group each Thursday morning to learn a new spiritual practice and spend time together practicing it. Using the *Spiritual Practices Handbook* by Adele Ahlberg Calhoun (IVP Press, 2015) as a guide, the group worked through a new practice each week and gradually built up a bank of practices that participants could draw from and use.

Over time, the group grew to include people from other congregations and friends with no congregational ties. Learning contemplative prayer, lectio divina and dozens of other practices over time proved to be life-giving and spiritually fulfilling. By working with the whole group and also using breakout rooms online, people could learn together, practice with another person and have meaningful experiences. It would have been almost impossible to bring together a group like this in a physical setting each week. But online with good leadership, the group proved to be an important new ministry. Online efforts to gather people for spiritual formation are just one way to take what has been a niche within the church and expand it to include more and more people.

As a result of online groups like this, hybrid congregations find themselves providing opportunities to gather people who might not have known each other outside of the online community. Over the course of time, these people may come to care for one another quite deeply and expand their sense of genuine community.

As you explore this for yourselves, remember that you don't have to do this alone and that congregations can partner to create a catalogue of increasingly helpful options where people can learn and grow. The staff and lay leaders in smaller congregations may only offer a limited number of educational and spiritual growth programs like Sunday School options for children and youth or educational experiences for adults, but if a cluster of congregations is confident enough to share programming, they can each offer coordinated options with an array of Bible classes, forums, spiritual growth opportunities and special worship experiences. The only barriers are the levels of trust and imagination that leaders provide.

Using Online Resources

One other rich opportunity offered by the hybrid church in spiritual formation, is the opportunity to assess and use a wide variety of resources and programs which are present online. With podcasts, videos, and so many things online – many of them excellent - for years, people have had access to hundreds of thousands of potential resources and tools for spiritual formation. But some are clearly better than others and guidance and leadership can really matter.

Practicing a hybrid model for spiritual formation will challenge congregations to serve as curators who point people toward useful online resources while also developing ways to use them in a learning community. Yes, there is a lot of poorly conceived stuff out there to sort through, but there are also many great resources for spiritual formation online. More good quality material is available online now than was available in any form just a decade or two ago! And the number of great resources is increasing more rapidly than anyone can keep up with.

These resources are almost always better when they are used and practiced in relationship with others. Most people learn best in community because they gain new insights and points of view from each other and because they can support and encourage each other and hold each other accountable to learning and practicing spiritual disciplines. So helping people find good resources to support spiritual growth and equipping people to connect with and support each other as they do means that for very little money, many groups can explore meaningful and creative options in high quality ways. The hybrid church ultimately seeks to use these as a way to gather in community and build relationships, to employ them as resources for faith formation and to multiply the opportunities for people to grow into the image of Christ for the sake of others.

In practicing spiritual formation, the hybrid church which embraces "both/and practices for ministry rather than "either/or" will be most likely to flourish. Congregations do not need to choose in-person over online opportunities for spiritual formation but instead see the value of both. Communities of faith that find ways to integrate online and on-the-ground activity into their shared life together will lead the whole church into a more integrated and holistic way of working – wherever the point of contact and activity may be.

We now live in a time where we have been presented with an opportunity to live more fully and faithfully into our calling to make disciples, and to discover that the ends of the earth have shifted to new places and connected in new ways. We are being invited to meet people in the various settings available to us and to use this new season in our life and ministry to fully engage the whole people of God. As Saint Paul writes, "I have become all things to all people, so that I might by any means save some" (I Corinthians 9:22, NRSV).

For Reflection and Discussion

Scripture: John 15:1-8

"I am the true vine, and my Father is the farmer. Every branch in me that doesn't bear fruit, he takes away. Every branch that bears fruit, he prunes, that it may bear more fruit. You are already pruned clean because of the word which I have spoken to you. Remain in me, and I in you. As the branch can't bear fruit by itself unless it remains in the vine, so neither can you, unless you remain in me. I am the vine. You are the branches. He who remains in me and I in him bears much fruit, for apart from me you can do nothing. If a man doesn't remain in me, he is thrown out as a branch and is withered; and they gather them, throw them into the fire, and they are burned. If you remain in me, and my words remain in you, you will ask whatever you desire, and it will be done for you.

In this my Father is glorified, that you bear much fruit; and so you will be my disciples.

Questions

1. In the text above, Jesus is clear that our fruitfulness as Christians is dependent (entirely) on our connections to him.

   a. How clear do you think this is in your own mind?

   b. Based on how people participate in the life of the church in things that enhance spiritual growth and discipleship, how clear do you think this is in the congregation as a whole? Give examples where you can.

2. What are the current practices you use regularly and personally to help you grow as a follower of Jesus?

3. Share stories of what your congregation has done to encourage faith formation either on the on-the-ground or online, or both.

4. Think about small groups in your setting. What ones exist and what percentage of people are involved? Is this an area where online attention could help start some new ways to gather people together?

5. What next steps might your congregation make to explore for expanding your practices and opportunities for spiritual formation both on-the-ground and/or online?

Prayer

God who calls, in Christ you have invited us to be disciples of Jesus and brought us into a journey that brings life to us and then through us to others. Help us to stay passionate about our connection to Christ and diligent in our walk as his followers. Help us cultivate an environment in our congregation's ministry where all hear the call of Jesus to follow him and all are able to respond through the work of the Spirit to walk life's path with him. Empower us, as we reflect on new ways to do ministry, to learn and grow and help others learn and grow as well. We pray this in the name of the one who has offered us the gift of life, Jesus Christ our Savior and Lord. Amen

5

Servanthood in the Hybrid Church

In 2006, I (Richard) felt called to go Biloxi, Mississippi, in response to the devastation from Hurricane Katrina. I had never traveled to assist with disaster recovery before and I had no idea what I would do when I got there, but I tentatively shared my plans with two trusted church members. The two of them decided to go as well and that is how my first mission trip to Biloxi began. It started with a personal sense of call and then included two people who felt the same desire to serve that I did. In no time at all, we had fourteen people going to Biloxi, and were accompanied by others who were willing to pray for us from home and help support our trip.

We arrived late on a Sunday night. The next morning, our team went in three different directions with a few of us assigned to the unglamorous job of moving a large supply tent a few feet from its original location. This was a big job and it took us most of the morning. As we were gasping for breath, a staff member looked at our work and said, "No, I think it was better where it was." We then put it back where it had been.

At that moment, one of my parishioners turned to me and said, "This is another fine mess you've gotten me into."

vered. "This is another fine
ˍˍ nas gotten us into."

The call to be engaged in servanthood is an essential part of who we are as people of God – it is something that God gets us into. As we consider the evolving nature of our shared ministry in the hybrid church, we discover that the landscape of our ministry is changing. The church will need to experiment and practice some trial and error as we seek to serve God and one another. We may find ourselves routinely saying, "This is a fine mess that God has gotten us into," while striving to remain gracious with one another.

Serving on-the-ground

One reason that service may be a more challenging area for a congregation that is on-the-ground and trying to do more online is the fact that service is often viewed as being the "hands of Christ." But how does a church think about the online world as a way to enhance the call to continue the ministry of Jesus and to live out our lives together in service to our neighbors?

First, remember that a hybrid church takes BOTH on-the-ground and online ministry seriously. So, physically present acts of service continue to be an essential part of the church. We aren't leaving behind the physical for the online world. We are functioning in both. So, some of those acts of service may not require a radical departure from ways that have been used before. In these instances, online resources can simply be used to enhance awareness, connection and communication in ways that strengthen the life of the church.

64

Echoes is an ecumenical church in Bellingham, Washington. They have organized around a principle of multiple, smaller-scaled worship experiences that are offered weekly and led by one of their team of part-time leaders. Every week they have indoor worship experiences, an outdoor wild church service and a creative worship service grounded in use of the arts. Each of these worship services is unique, but also a part of the whole. Over time, many worshippers gravitate toward a particular worship service yet clearly remain part of the whole.

The congregation works hard to connect and mobilize people online because of this dynamic. Pastor Charis Weathers says, "We have multiple worship experiences but this is still one community. We have one email list, one social media site (Facebook), one web site, and that's how we inform and invite people to participate in service."

The primary place that the congregation facilitates servanthood takes place in what Echoes calls "Service Church." This monthly effort invites everyone to join in working on a service project, often in partnership with other local groups or organizations. The work is still hands-on, but much of the organizing and communicating happens using online tools and communication.

This is a good example of a congregation working online to communicate with and mobilize people for physical service on-the-ground. It is obviously a way of working that most congregations have already experienced to a certain degree – the key is increasing proficiency and engagement. At least it isn't a huge paradigm shift!

Online groups as servant basecamps

Service can also happen a little differently because relationships and the work of planning in a hybrid congregation have relocated to online, in part. Online small groups using tools like Google Hangouts and Zoom have become widely accepted and are now a permanent part of the church world. More and more groups will be fostering hybrid experiences with part of a group physically present while others connect using technology. In addition, small groups and teams choose to meet online for almost everything. It has made it easier to be together, taken less time and proven useful. The permanent presence of online gatherings changes where relationships can be nurtured, sustained and mobilized.

One congregation decided to organize online small groups based on their desire to deepen their faith in God and grow in their ability to serve others. Among the groups they formed are a group focused on Racial Justice, another on LGBTQIA+ Celebration and Ally Support, and another focused on Caring for Creation. These groups grew out of the passions of their congregation and their online community as well as people's desire to learn how to serve more fully. It offers a wholistic way of being together that incorporates online gatherings and creates opportunities for service – online and on-the-ground.

The beauty of this congregation's ministry is their ability to build community among their members and friends and to equip them for ongoing ministry together in their daily lives.

In these cases, where most of the participants are gathering online but still within reasonable geographic distances of each other, teams and small groups can be equipped and encouraged to include service in their team's commitment and identity. That has been a common practice of small groups prior to online ministry being the meeting place. Groups convening online can reflect together on their own passions and connections, determine what they would like to do to serve together in meaningful and needed ways, and then physically gather to work at a food pantry, participate in a Habitat for Humanity build project, or engage in whatever service they have mutually decided to take on. In other words, literally *everything* leading up to the act of service including planning and relationships will take place online, but the acts of service will happen on-the-ground.

Here the key is leadership keeping a theology and culture of service before the congregation as a whole and developing a shared accountability to ensure that groups retain service in their shared life together. Although it might be easy for an online group to forget this, meeting online does not remove the call to service; it simply becomes another place where that call can be issued and answered. As one pastor we talked to about service in a hybrid church reminded us, "Part of our mission statement states that we exist to help create a better community in the world around us." Of course, if this is true then it is equally true whether a group is physically together or meeting online.

Larger Scale Service Opportunities

Another level of online work moves service to something more widely dispersed. All around the country (and the world) are places where important service opportunities exist, many of which lie out of reach or the imagination for some congregational members.

A good example of this on an ecumenical level is the CROP Walk, an annual event to raise awareness and resources for hunger. Historically, participants have asked for commitments to sponsor their efforts as they walk. Then, at a given date, time and location all the participants in a particular area have met, had some sort of sendoff, and walked a route en masse, raising funds and awareness as they do.

The pandemic meant that this kind of huge event was not an option, at least for a while – groups had to figure out how to adjust. "Virtual CROP Walks" popped up and many walks took place in new ways. People signed up to walk online, requested pledges almost exclusively using social media, and then often walked their own route at a time that worked for them – reporting to their supporters that it was happening. In some cases, a local congregation could schedule its own team to walk at a time that worked for them. Now that this format is in place, future options for expanding the CROP Walk to being online will surely continue well into the future. If done well, more people will be reached, and more resources will be raised than the previous on-the-ground only methods could have done.

Entering the online world opens up a multitude of possibilities never before available. For example, online requests from organizations are increasingly finding their way out to the world due to web sites becoming more engaging and invitational. Animal shelters need chew toys that can be made from old T-shirts, cancer patients benefit from hand-written cards with words of encouragement, critical issues call for widespread advocacy and the list goes on and on.

People can do things in their own home, gathered in someone's garage or as a group in a church meeting room and send the results of their labors to people and places where they are then used and where people are eager and grateful for the partnership. While this used to be limited to things like making and sending quilts (still a needed effort), the online world has opened up a wider range of opportunities and needs for people to respond to. It also opens up an awareness that diverse skills and abilities are valuable and can be put to use in serving our neighbor. It may be that going online can expand and deepen a culture of service.

Actual service online

What is also rapidly changing is the fact that more and more *actual service can happen online*. The online world has been transforming from a communications tool to an increasingly robust place for life to happen. Advocacy work can happen online. Actions by community organizing groups can be organized and take place online. And actual service projects can happen online. While we won't try to take up too much space with stories and examples, just one might be helpful to start you thinking.

Librivox is an online provider of audiobooks to the public – specifically developed to get more people access to audiobooks for learning and edification. They only work with public domain works and they produce these to create a complete online audiobook library. Their entire project and one hundred percent the of volunteer service happens online. Using the material from their web site at librivox.org, here is a summary of how a project happens:

- a book coordinator posts a book in the New Projects Launch Pad Section.

- a meta coordinator claims the project and moves the thread to the appropriate forum.

- volunteers "claim" chapters to read.

- the readers record their chapters in digital format.

- the book coordinator collects all the files of all the chapters.

- the book coordinator sends the collected files to a meta coordinator.

- we check the files for technical problems in the Listeners Wanted section.

- the book coordinator sends the collected, corrected files to a meta coordinator.

- another public domain audiobook is made available for free.

This is an example of a project done *totally* online – no one ever is physically in the presence of anyone else for the entire project. Most participants helping make it happen will never meet one another. But together something remarkable and good happens and people with reading and vision problems have access to all sorts of good material.

These same kinds of innovations are making mentoring in

schools, visiting in prisons and caring for people in times of struggle or isolation expand as online visiting and interaction make it possible to go more easily where we could not go before. In doing so, the church can be a source of support and encouragement for people in all sorts of situations. This means more and more ways to serve will be online. Stay alert and your congregation may be able to venture into completely new areas of ministry not even dreamed of on-the-ground!

All of these approaches scratch the surface of how being a hybrid and a servant church are beginning to be lived out in new ways.

This is a chance to learn new ways of connecting with one another and serving our neighbors wherever they live – across the street or around the world. And while we are learning, becoming a hybrid church will multiply the ways we connect with one another and increase the opportunities for us to serve. The keys to making progress will be to notice what God is doing in our midst, cultivate meaningful relationships with our neighbors, continue to remain alert to what's happening in our context and recognize how we are called to respond as we learn from God and one another.

There will be times when the best and only way to learn is through trial and error. There will be times when all of us will find ourselves in the midst of something we could not have expected and say to God, "This is another fine mess you've gotten us into." In such moments, take a deep breath, smile and give thanks to God. In the discoveries that happen you are likely to be blessed in new and unexpected ways.

For Reflection and Discussion

Scripture: Mark 14:3-9

While he was at Bethany, in the house of Simon the leper, as he sat at the table, a woman came having an alabaster jar of ointment of pure nard—very costly. She broke the jar, and poured it over his head. But there were some who were indignant among themselves, saying, "Why has this ointment been wasted? For this might have been sold for more than three hundred denarii, and given to the poor." So they grumbled against her.

⁶ But Jesus said, "Leave her alone. Why do you trouble her? She has done a good work for me. ⁷ For you always have the poor with you, and whenever you want to, you can do them good; but you will not always have me. ⁸ She has done what she could. She has anointed my body beforehand for the burying. ⁹ Most certainly I tell you, wherever this Good News may be preached throughout the whole world, that which this woman has done will also be spoken of for a memorial of her."

Questions

1. In the text above, the woman comes to offer service to Jesus out of her deep love and commitment to him and in the process, she is rebuked by others. What is the most risky, challenging or controversial act of service you can remember your congregation being involved in?

2. What are the most meaningful service experiences you have had personally as a Christian?

3. In what ways does your congregation encourage, equip and facilitate people in acts of service?

4. Has your congregation ever offered any service opportunities that were significantly facilitated by online work or even totally online? During the time when the pandemic changed ministry, how did service change? Stay the same? Disappear?

5. In what ways might you be called to expand either/both your congregation's online or on-the-ground servant ministry?

Prayer

God of love, you call us to acts of love that involve more than feelings, but true actions for the sake of the neighbor. As we walk with and learn from Jesus, we see that this is truly part of the way you bring life to us and allow us to share life with others as well. As you call each of us to live lives filled with service, open our hearts and minds to not just do service, but be servants as part of the core of who we are. As we work to shape ministry in the church, help us to lead in ways that make service a deep and real part of each person's life, in the name of the one who came to serve all humanity, Jesus Christ our Lord. Amen

6

Evangelical Witness in the Hybrid Church

Before digging too deeply into witnessing in a hybrid congregation and reflecting on what issues and opportunities
going online bring, this is an important place to remember
what being an evangelical person is all about and what witnessing is. This is not primarily about a strategy to promote
the church. The church is called and formed by God to bear
witness to what God has done and is doing in the life, death
and resurrection of Jesus. That's why this chapter follows a
lot of other material on worship, small groups and spiritual
formation. This is not about just being better marketers,
although being better at sharing our message is essential. It
is also about being sure that what we share is the message
about God's saving acts in Jesus. God's invitation for us to
join in with God at work are at the heart of this message.

This means being an effective online church will require us to
do whatever remedial work is needed with people to have a
better awareness of the good news, a solid theology grounded in grace, and a strong belief that God uses our witness
as a vehicle to faith and faithfulness. But the ultimate work
belongs to God and flows from the belief and awareness that

God's actions are not just past tense but present tense – the risen Christ is alive and at work in our world today. There is ample evidence that these barometers are under-functioning in many faithful church attenders. The desire to witness online offers new opportunities to do faith formation and faith sharing with greater intentionality. This can and must benefit people's understanding of God in their lives regardless of whether they are online or not; it can and should find its way into both physical and online interactions.

When Jesus said, "You will be my witnesses…" (Acts 1:8), he was calling the church that would be birthed by the Holy Spirit at Pentecost to stay grounded and focused on God's saving work in Christ. This core is the only core that makes all the work we do as a church "evangelical." While the word has taken on too many other meanings in our divided public sphere, at its center, to be evangelical is to be committed to sharing Christ in ways that bring *good news* to the hearers. Online or not, this is essential.

Many mainline congregations were already lacking real intentionality about witnessing and being an invitational community on-the-ground. This is only compounded as we now live into new models for ministry. As congregations shift from a purely on-site ministry into a hybrid model, the call to intentional and faithful witness becomes even more critical for the future work of the church.

In fact, sales of my (Dave) best-selling book, *The Invitational Christian*, almost came to a screeching halt for the first few months when the COVID-19 shutdown happened. Over time, sales began to increase again as people began to wrap their head around things. Some of this was a preoccupation with doing what needed to be done just to find our way online, but some was also due to the thinking that, "If we can't go to church for worship, then how on earth can we invite others to join us there?" If we struggle to imagine inviting people in a world we know, consider how much more we struggle to invite people when we are functioning in a new and quickly changing world!

The reality is being online doesn't take away opportunities for witness, evangelism and being invitational – it expands them. Congregations that take being online seriously and being on-the-ground seriously will find new doorways opening to them. The interactions in and between the online world and the on-the-ground world will bring many new ways of engaging people.

The word *engagement* is an important one. It has always been an important principle. Quite simply, we cannot truly bear witness to Christ without being engaged with other people. There is a proactive and real connection that is made and relationships are furthered when people authentically engage one another. Being online doesn't change this fundamental reality – it only emphasizes it. This is essential – evangelical witness is about people not programs.

In some ways, this focus on people can be a healthy reminder. I (Dave) have done all sorts of consulting work with congregations over the past two decades. I can't tell you how many times that we have had people gather in small groups and dig into their thoughts about an issue, reflect on their faith stories or share something meaningful about themselves. Very often I hear the same thing over and over again: "I have known (person's name) for so long and you know, I had no idea about that. I had never heard that story." In fact, I have had spouses say that about each other!

Sadly, the truth is that often in the physically gathered church people who see each other week after week for years sometimes never get much deeper awareness of each other than they had developed in the first few months. This isn't to say these relationships aren't important – of course they are. But many of our gatherings don't help people dig deeper as much as sustain what is. We can definitely do a better job on-the-ground of helping people reflect on their faith stories, share them with each other and discover together how the God who has come to us in Jesus is at work in and among them. Don't assume that the move to online means doing less work on-the-ground. Both arenas need attention if we are to become a more evangelical community where the good news of God's grace and love in Jesus are lifted up graciously and lovingly by God's people. The chance to work online is a chance to look at foundations for faithful and authentic witnessing and build a whole new and more effective church for the next chapter of our unfolding history.

New Ways to Invite

At the same time, going online opens up a lot of new possibilities. If people are strategic and committed to being effective witnesses for Christ, some of the things that made people tentative in a physical environment are easily overcome in an online one. Because the online world is only as "real" as the engagement points, fear of rejection online is often reduced. People often chickened out when speaking in person was the primary avenue. Many people report feeling like they should have said something and even wanted to say something in some previous conversation(s). But they couldn't find the words or bring themselves to do it. Some even report feeling guilty at their failures to speak. But online, people can share ideas and post comments, as long as they are gracious about it, and others will see them.

In addition, online witnessing gives people time to frame their thoughts or borrow from others. While you might be afraid of tripping over your words if you have to say them out loud when you are a bit nervous, you can take your time, edit your thoughts and write things out ahead before you post something online. When my (Dave's) wife wants to write out a nice note in a greeting card, she often takes a piece of paper and writes and edits a draft until she feels that she has it right. Then she copies it neatly in the card with the confidence that she has said what she wants to say and done it well. Online posts give us the same opportunity. People can write and edit until they are happy with the message and then hit "post."

Because the world of social media is a mix of private and public, people also have the freedom to go narrow and connect with an individual person or go wider and connect with a broader group of people. Both are important and helping people think about social media and how to use it can be really helpful.

For example, one way to invite a person physically is a one-to-one invitation, whether shared orally or through a written card. In either case, the person inviting initiates the invitation and offers to an invitee a chance to respond and come with them to something – it may be worship, a service opportunity, a small group, a meal or any one of many things. If done well, this is probably an invitation that takes place within the framework of an existing relationship. Perhaps the people have talked together about faith or life issues in some ways that give context for the invitation and therefore it is not just a cold invitation out of the blue but a warm one based on awareness of the person. This is the healthiest invitation, in most cases.

The online world is no different. An open invitation is possible and will likely do no harm while generating some responses. People can join you in an online thing like a live stream of your worship because they risk less online than they do in person. They feel less awkward, can watch from home and can simply leave for another web location if they find it boring or irrelevant. So posts like "Join us for online worship this Sunday" are probably more effective than walking door-to-door and hanging flyers that say, "Join us for worship this Sunday" when that response commitment requires entering a strange building, sitting with new people and not feeling like you can just stand up and leave after 15 minutes if the experience isn't what you hoped it would be. "Dropping in" online is more likely to happen, particularly if someone sees the online invitation on the timeline of someone they know and already like or trust.

But there are additional online tools that can increase your ability to move beyond basic invitations. Social media sites each have their own ways to expand the reach beyond a generic post. Sharing a post, promoting an event and even paying for ways to boost the likelihood that an online piece of information is seen and shared expand your options. While this chapter will not dig deeply into how each platform works, know that Facebook, Instagram, YouTube, Twitter, Vimeo and other sites have their own ways to share and promote material. Teaching people how each platform works and how to use it well will greatly enhance the ability of the church to get its message out and to engage new people in new ways.

Equipping People

This means that one key part of having an online church presence is to equip people to be effective at living and connecting in their own online circles – person to person sharing of faith and invitations. This goes without saying at one level, but for decades the church has wished people would physically invite people to join them in congregational life and ministry yet done little to equip them to actually do it. It has been assumed that it is simple and people would just figure it out. In most cases that meant disappointing results.

The strong response to *The Invitational Christian* showed that people need and want straightforward help inviting people on-the-ground. While most church leaders wished and may have even encouraged people to invite, statistics show that well over 9 out of 10 people almost never do. They either didn't feel enough confidence about the church to believe they had something to share, or they didn't feel passionate enough about it to overcome their fears and then share it and invite others to join them. Being a hybrid church does not mean abandoning face-to-face witness and invitation. Being hybrid means doing both face-to-face and online witness and invitation. Don't abandon one important place in hopes that moving online will simply solve the issue. It won't. But it can be a place of making our witness stronger in ways that impact both our physical gatherings and our online connections.

Collectively, the congregation can be a catalyst for this to happen in ways that help people grow personally and share faith with others, often at the same time. Congregational leaders should take advantage of the ability to engage people meaningfully and in their own time apart from Sundays. Blogs, event postings, photos with captions grounded in scripture, questions to post and share can all be useful at encouraging the faith of physical participants in their online world. These can then be shared and find their way onto the screens of friends, family, neighbors and coworkers who are connected online. Something that encourages a person with deep faith may be the spark that the Spirit uses to form new faith in someone else. Because such posts are already written (hopefully well) and theologically vetted by church leaders, they become good teaching and reinforcement for people who participate already and a faithful witness to others outside our current congregational circle.

Teaching people how to connect scripture and everyday experiences helps equip them with a better lens for seeing God at work in and around them. While finding the right words on the spot may be daunting and seem impossible to some people, the chance to write something and post it online with a photo that uses God language will allow many of our people to articulate a story or self-understanding that they would have otherwise missed out on in a physical context. These kinds of posts bear witness to faith in the God who has come to us in Jesus. Done well, and with an alertness to how people respond and how to be appropriately invitational, they are an important way for each person to be a more evangelical presence.

One final thought for this chapter that is essential to remember: For most of us, being a hybrid church means functioning faithfully and effectively online and on-the-ground. Both environments need to be viewed as meaningful, real and important. In a healthy witnessing congregation, this means that witness and invitation is connecting both worlds in various ways, depending on the connections and life realities of the people we meet. There is not a one-size-fits-all balance for everyone. Some people will be mostly living in our online world. Some will be living mostly within physical gatherings. But viewing it as a whole, many will be living and reflecting on faith and being a part of Christ's Church in both places.

You may meet someone online who lives far away, build meaningful connections with them and they will end up inviting then into and engaging their faith life through your congregation's ministry online with no ability to ever physically show up because they live so far away. Live with it – it's OK! It also means you may have some people, often but not always older members, who have physical patterns, needs and desires that make meeting in person their primary or only way of being church. Live with it – it's also OK!

Many people, if not most, will be active in a mix of things. Perhaps someone comes to worship on-the-ground the first time, wants to be in a small group but has a small child and their spouse isn't interested in church life at all (yet). They may want to come to worship and be physically present, bring their child and be together with people in person. But coming physically for a small group during the week probably won't work for them and might be viewed as a burden by their spouse, so an online Zoom session is perfect for studying, sharing and getting to connect with people during the week. They participate in worship in one way and deepen faith and connections in another. That's OK, too! Because effective evangelical witness is about both sharing the gospel and inviting people into a life of faith, whatever onramps work for people to grow in faith are the right ones.

In all of this, being hybrid means being nimble, flexible and relationally alert. It means remembering that the goal of evangelical witness is to provide a faithful connection to the ongoing story of God in Christ and then allowing the Holy Spirit to work – online and face-to-face.

Invitations open doors for people to take another step in their journeys. And it means praying that whatever we do, we do it well and trust God will use our endeavors to bring newfound faith and increasing faithfulness to the people we encounter – wherever we meet them.

For Reflection and Discussion

Scripture: John 4:26-29, 39-42

Jesus said to her, "I am he, the one who speaks to you." At this, his disciples came. They marveled that he was speaking with a woman; yet no one said, "What are you looking for?" or, "Why do you speak with her?" So the woman left her water pot, went away into the city, and said to the people, "Come, see a man who told me everything that I did. Can this be the Christ?"

...From that city many of the Samaritans believed in him because of the word of the woman, who testified, "He told me everything that I did." So when the Samaritans came to him, they begged him to stay with them. He stayed there two days. Many more believed because of his word. They said to the woman, "Now we believe, not because of your speaking; for we have heard for ourselves, and know that this is indeed the Christ, the Savior of the world."

Questions

1. In the text above, the woman shared her excitement about Jesus with the people in her town. Who are the people in your life responsible for you hearing about and trusting in Jesus?

2. In what ways have you practiced being an been a witness for Christ, both in congregational life and in your personal life? How easy is it for you to use words to share the story and how much do you struggle to do so?

3. How is bearing witness to what God is doing through Jesus Christ different from "promoting" your congregation? Which is easier for you and why?

4. If you think about ministry in your congregation, what are the things that would help a new person grow deeper spiritually or find connections to what God is doing in ways that give them a sense of purpose or meaning?

5. What is one aspect of your congregation's evangelical witness which might require the most attention at this time? What are some necessary action steps you will need to take to make this possible? (i.e. budget adjustments, staff or volunteer commitments, training opportunities, adjusting priorities for time, energy and resources)

Prayer

God of love, your deep compassion for the human family meant that you have come down to us, reaching out with love and offering us the costly grace of the cross. So we come to you in thanks for your coming in Christ. Fill us with the excitement of the woman at the well, so that we are able to share our faith with others and invite them to come and see what we have come to see in Jesus. May we find ways to use new ways of working to share the message of life and the good news of Jesus, in whose name we pray. Amen

7

Pastoral and Congregational Care in the Hybrid Church

We are called to love one another — there is no getting around that central truth.

A benefit of having to be more intentional about congregational care is that it gives leaders a chance to remind everyone of the core foundations of congregational care. 1 John 4:19 tells us, "We love because he first loved us." Congregational care is rooted in the love we receive from God in Christ. We are not simply a random group of secular humanists doing this because it is a good idea. We are the people of God and the body of Christ. We do this because of who God is. We do this because of who we are.

Martin Luther built on this idea when he said, "It is the duty of all Christians to be Christ for their neighbor." The care people offer is from God. It embodies the actions of a God who takes up residence in disciples who then live out Christ's ongoing work in their actions with and toward others. Whatever care we provide for one another in whatever medium, we are called to measure our care through the call to love one another.

One aspect of church life that was especially challenged during the COVID-19 pandemic was pastoral and congregational care. Care which had happened naturally within the flow of congregational life could not happen in the same way since people could not be in the same physical space together without taking substantial risks. People who had attended worship on Sunday usually sat in the same pews, interacted with the same people and felt connected as a result. All of the care that was offered in the natural flow of congregational life – fellowship and refreshments, storytelling, passing the peace, getting a hug, etc. – disappeared at once.

Then as awareness and creativity permitted people to discover paths forward, previous practices were slowly modified or restored, and new practices were developed. The struggles related to the pandemic were an opportunity to get a glimpse of how we will provide congregational care in the future. As Father John Baldovin observed, this "crisis has shown us people's hunger for faith." (Quoted by Kerry Webber in "Social Distancing and the Sacraments," America Magazine Online, May 17, 2020). People have always been hungry for God, but a crisis often makes some of us more keenly aware of that than before. It has challenged the church to provide care that is both faithful and adaptive to our current and emerging contexts.

But a hybrid church is not a pandemic church. It is a church that is moving into the future, catapulted into that future from the pandemic into new ways of being church together. Some things will be changed in ways yet to be discovered, but the changes will impact how people interact with and care for each other. This will include how the pastor and church staff do this work as well as how lay members interact and care for each other.

A new intentionality

A hybrid congregation will have to be much more intentional at how it provides for pastoral and congregational care. The things that happened naturally when physical gathering was the primary medium will still happen in some circles but not happen in the same way in others. If a church is creating a sense of community online, how is that different than the way we created a sense of community on-the-ground? Will people who primarily participate online interact with people who primarily participate by being physically present? Or will the two realms of work remain somewhat separated in practice? Will a crisis in the life of someone who participates primarily online lead to pastoral and congregational care that is offered by being physically present for that person? The list of questions and unknowns goes on and on. A hybrid church will not assume that a person's primary medium of participation limits the options for caring for them when they have a significant need. It will ask and imagine, "How can this be done best?"

Of course, in a hybrid congregation, much caregiving is retained among those who participate in the on-the-ground ministries of the congregation. While interactions may change from the pre-COVID church, many of the benefits of being in the same place on a regular basis are still there and are intrinsic in being together and being human. People will see each other, spend time together and build meaningful, caring, long-term relationships. If clergy and lay leaders are alert during these gatherings, the ability to connect and interact with a higher percentage of the people who are present may even be enhanced, since current trends show that gatherings may be smaller than before and allow for increased interpersonal awareness.

Marshal McLuhan famously said that "the medium is the message." We have always assumed that physical presence was the gold standard for pastoral and congregational care. Hybrid congregations will have plenty of opportunities to do on-the-ground pastoral and congregational care, but they will also stretch to include new ways. Whatever medium they use to provide care, whether it is a physical visit, a phone call, text message, an online video session or Facebook post – it should be seen as an expression of love. What matters is that it is offered faithfully with awareness of the people in our care and the situation in which we serve.

Using the online world as a place for caring for one another opens lots of new possibilities for the church in the future. Many life passages went online during the COVID crisis as congregations developed the ability to use online meeting platforms to host weddings, stream funerals and include family in baptisms. This frequently required immense creativity, careful conversations and lots of patience as people navigated these experiments in real time. They also produced innovative and often satisfying results, some of which are a basis for working in new ways in the future.

A hybrid church will not say, "Now we don't have to do that anymore." Instead it will say, "What did we learn by doing that and how will it allow us to connect with and care for more people at this important time in their lives?" Hybrid events will allow physical and online connections to happen simultaneously, often in new and creative ways that increase connections and offer a genuine sense of care and compassion. That's because we have opened up new doors using different tools. When we try to close those doors and go back to the old "normal" we do so to our peril. Now every on-the-ground life passage (baptisms, weddings, funerals, confirmations, etc.) invites the question, "If we stream this or include an online component, can we involve people who could not have been included or do ministry in a new and better way as we do it?"

Increased Ways to Care
Some New and Some Old

Technology offers new tools to remember everyone in our circle of care. One congregation we know has a subscription to an e-card site. The site allows for cards to be selected, notes included and dates preset for them to be sent automatically. The office staff have compiled a list of every member whose birthday and email address are on file and each month they set up all the cards to be sent to members and other participants. On the day of the birthday, the card is delivered by email and the person gets a card from their church family online. Adding this practice means every person receives a contact on their birthday. The responses received indicate that that these e-cards from the church are noticed and appreciated – they express caring and connection effectively. The same practice can be done for baptismal anniversaries, wedding anniversaries and other events – as expansive and personal as makes sense in a given context. This and other online tools make options for caring for everyone more efficient and offer important expressions of connection and concern. Be sure to stay abreast of other online tools to remember people as individuals in simple yet powerful ways.

At the same time, we are seeing a helpful trend in hand-written notes that are delivered by snail mail. Church leaders who take the time to thank people when they do good work, congratulate people when they accomplish something important or comfort people in their sorrow rarely regret the time it takes to handwrite and mail a note or card. Being a hybrid church may catapult us forward, but it also calls us to be mindful of all the tools available to us for expressing care. Very little can beat the feeling of mattering that happens when someone opens a first-class envelope and finds a personal note written especially for them. Some of the most effective ministries in the future will be using both the most up to date online tools and old-fashioned paper and pen.

Increasing options for how to care also creates the possibility of a much wider variety in ways of exhibiting that care. Each person's soul has a character – knowing the person well and using the appropriate tools we have to care for each person is a gift. In the Gospels, we see that Jesus rarely heals any two people in the same way. Sometimes he simply said a word of healing without visiting the sick person. Other times he touched them, laid hands on them or even spit! In the same way, the care we offer for one another should reflect that no two individuals or situations are ever exactly the same.

As many pastors can tell you, some parishioners appreciate visits in their homes while others would be horrified if you dropped by. Others clearly prefer to meet in the office or at a coffee shop. Still others simply want a phone call or text message. A high percentage of people view social media interactions as central and an ever-growing number of people prefer to meet or connect electronically. New groups can and will form online; new people will join the system who don't have any memory of previous ways of caring, and with that blank slate comes a new openness to new ways of working.

Working in this way means seeing people sharing a physical visit, speaking with people over the phone, sending text messages and emails, and using digital communication such as Zoom to visit in ways that allow us to see each other while recognizing that we may not always be able to be or desire to be physically present. In a hybrid church, we use all of the tools at our disposal to enhance contact and build caring relationships over time so that we can be present for one another when needs arise. In the process, the toolkit of ways to interact with people throughout congregational life is expanded.

New trends in the healthcare industry can be a helpful model for the church to learn from. It has made radical shifts to use technology well, work more efficiently and be more focused on the patient. Many of the same concepts can also help the church envision pastoral and congregational care in new ways for a new future. Telehealth uses a mix of online/phone apps and videoconferencing to help monitor a patient's health remotely. Telehealth is focused on the care of the whole person, and this has become an increasingly important part of our health care system, accelerating the ways in which we have adapted to providing and receiving healthcare online. Both authors have used this with excellent experiences and other people we know have been surprised to discover that they have received remarkably effective care online too. In some cases, healthcare specialties like counseling have found that some people actually prefer meeting online to meeting physically. And some have found this model to be empowering since it allows them more direct access and a more active role in their own care.

These ideas help us think about how we can provide pastoral care and counseling in the future. In many cases, we find that people are grateful for the opportunity to meet online with their pastor or a church care team member and may even prefer it. At the same time, this allows staff to visit more people and spend quality time with them with no commute times between visits.

Congregational Care
Everyone's Responsibility

The availability of so many mediums is also accelerating another important shift happening in the church. That is the change from the language of "pastoral" care to "congregational" care. This shift becomes even more helpful and necessary as we live into the emerging model of the hybrid church. For many years, it was assumed that caring for the sick and homebound members of a congregation was the work of the clergy. When other members did visit, they were often seen as "helping the pastor," and sometimes their visits were even discounted as secondary to a "real visit" with the pastor.

This way of understanding care has often failed to appreciate the gifts of all the baptized people of God and the call that we love one another. This does not mean that clergy should no longer care for church members, but that they serve within the community of the faithful while also equipping others to share this same ministry. Congregational care is ultimately the work of the whole priesthood of believers.

While the presence of ministries like Stephen's Ministers and Befrienders has not been uncommon, a joyful surprise is emerging as congregations are forming or expanding their care teams and ministering to one another in new ways.

People are discovering that they interact with each other more in the hybrid congregation than they had before. Many are noticing that they have the ability to provide increased points of personal contact through social media posts and messaging, gathering online for midweek prayer and the formation of online Bible studies and small groups. Equipping a team of people to interact and be alert to peoples' presence in online ministry can cause caring to take on whole new dimensions. Good congregational care, on-the-ground and online, is the work of the whole congregation. Moving beyond paid staff to include well prepared lay leaders is both essential and an incredible opportunity.

Finally, remember that pastoral and congregational care also happen at online gatherings that may be categorized in your mind as "spiritual formation" but which offer a chance for people to gather online, share updates on life and pray for each other together. People who never could find the time when commuting was mandatory now gladly make the time to connect with congregational life throughout the week. This is enabling a new sense of connection and community within the congregation. What used to happen at a table in the fellowship hall after Sunday worship may be happening online during the week in new ways. Wise leaders ensure that this is included, not by accident or default, but with some intentionality whenever and however people gather in a hybrid environment. And wise leaders make sure that the whole people of God are equipped to offer Christian care and compassion online, to ongoing members of the church as well as to new people who "wander in" online.

It is striking to recognize that digital communication has been an intrinsic part of our lives for years, but the church has often been reluctant to embrace new technology and ways of communicating into our ministries. Moving forward, much will depend on our ability to adapt our expectations to a changing context and to communicate well so people can participate in developing new ways of caring in the church and own the new reality as it unfolds. The "new normal" will continue to evolve in ways we cannot fully predict, but these changing realities hold great potential and, as God always does, God will ultimately find new ways of sharing love among Christ's people by using them.

For Reflection and Discussion

Scripture: John 15:9-17

Even as the Father has loved me, I also have loved you. Remain in my love. If you keep my commandments, you will remain in my love; even as I have kept my Father's commandments, and remain in his love. I have spoken these things to you, that my joy may remain in you, and that your joy may be made full.

[12] "This is my commandment, that you love one another, even as I have loved you. Greater love has no one than this, that someone lay down his life for his friends. You are my friends, if you do whatever I command you. No longer do I call you servants, for the servant doesn't know what his lord does. But I have called you friends, for everything that I heard from my Father, I have made known to you. You didn't choose me, but I chose you and appointed you, that you should go and bear fruit, and that your fruit should remain; that whatever you will ask of the Father in my name, he may give it to you.

"I command these things to you, that
you may love one another.

Questions

1. Jesus tells his disciples that they are to "love one another, even as I have loved you." How has love and/or the lack of it influenced your relationship with Christ over time? How has it impacted your involvement in Christ's church?

2. What are the core assumptions that inform your congregation's understanding of pastoral and congregational care? In other words, what do most people expect in these areas?

3. What has been your personal experience of pastoral or congregational care using any kinds of technology (phone call, text, email, ecards, online conversations, etc.)? Do you think that if the situation was right, you could find increased use of these as helpful for you or would you be more likely to find it inadequate? Why?

4. If you were to enhance one area of pastoral or congregational care using the kinds of material discussed in this chapter, what improvements could you make, or ideas could you implement to improve how your congregation expresses care for people?

Prayer

God of love, in Christ you demonstrate that you love us and call us to respond by loving one another. As the world changes and new ways to express care become both possible and necessary, help us to adapt to changing contexts and to adopt new ways of caring for one another, so that we might more fully be Christ for one another. It is in Christ's name that we pray. Amen

8

Stewardship in the Hybrid Church

Stewardship in the hybrid church starts with the same values at the core as all good stewardship work in the church. Stewardship has little to do with fundraising and everything to do with discipleship. It is less about collecting money and more about mobilizing resources for God's work. It is grounded in neither guilt nor duty but instead heavily focuses on gratitude and generosity. In the end, stewardship helps people who love Christ and see the church as continuing Christ's ministry in our time find ways to deepen that commitment and invest the resources at their disposal into the mission of God – in and through this faith community. Stewardship is always rooted in helping people see their lives as an extension of the life, death and resurrection of Jesus.

To help people grow in their stewardship commitments, we are committed to recommending some sort of checkup – at a minimum, reflecting annually on how giving fits into each person's way of following Jesus. Rethinking the annual stewardship campaign in this way can reframe this time in the church year from looking at how to increase giving to the church to being a checkup of the way generosity has been built into the lives of God's people. A framing question becomes, "If God is generous and at our best we look like God, how are you doing at reflecting the generosity of God in your own giving?" In this mindset, pledges are ended and personal goals are set; increasing donations is transformed into the opportunity to grow in generosity.

These are not just verbal techniques to see if people will respond to new language. They are genuinely changing the focus of stewardship from the needs of the institution to receive into a focus on the call of every follower of Jesus to give. When people remember that following Jesus encompasses every aspect of their lives, and when people are committed not just to keeping the organization going but to furthering the ministry of Jesus, then God will mobilize and provide the resources needed for committed people to do that work. That is a matter of faith and faithfulness.

Meeting goals in an online world

There are things about being a hybrid church that can transform how the church approaches this work as well as how it plays out in peoples' daily lives. For example, I can guarantee that almost every person who sets a giving goal for the year ahead can realize that goal. How many aspects of our life could ensure that kind of guarantee? Want to lose 20 pounds this year? How many people who say that actually make it happen? Not many. Want to learn a new language this year? Same answer – not many. The reason is that most challenging goals in our personal growth and development require an ongoing and persistent act of the will. Most people get excited about reaching a goal when they set it, but few people have the kind of support system and energy to sustain that for twelve months or longer.

This is where the online world can change everything about financial goals. Do you want to give a certain amount to the work of the church this year? Would you like to do it by giving weekly, twice a month or once a month? Divide your annual goal by the number of times you will give through the year, enter it in an online giving portal along with your banking information and allow your decision to happen. You did what you wanted and envisioned to do and can celebrate – your goal has been accomplished! Now pray about it again for the next year – does God want you to keep doing what you are doing or grow in some way? Let the answer to that prayer guide your giving goal for the year to come and do it again.

This kind of successful effort was challenging in an all on-the-ground church. A person could have good intentions and a genuine desire to grow but then the challenges of life each week make it difficult to manage weekly choices and paper transactions. For many people, bills after Christmas when credit card statements arrive might mean skipping a week or two with the hope of catching up later. Then a car repair in March means another reason to drop a week or two and plan to make it up later. A vacation over the summer involves two or three Sundays away and offerings are missed again. Under such conditions, someone could have good intentions to do better but be unable to make it actually happen.

A year end statement from the church would produce a list of perhaps forty or more weekly gifts that were right on target, and also end up short due to offerings that were missed for some reason. Although the ongoing self-perception would be that such people would have met their goal almost every week, the cumulative impact of Christmas bills, a car repair and a few weeks of vacation might add up to falling short by hundreds of dollars or more. The result? A hole too deep to make up within the cashflow of the family and a feeling of disappointment, failure and guilt. I have seen the kinds of demoralizing letters that people in these situations have received from pastors whose focus was on the wrong place – wanting the money to show up more than they wanted the spiritual wellbeing of the giver to increase.

New methods to engage people

The online world allows people to make real decisions and take real actions in ways that were not possible before. The truth is most people who love Christ and the church want to be generous and want to grow in faith and faithfulness. Online giving options provide new and more effective resources than had been previously available. People who can see, manage and measure growth are likely to celebrate that and rejoice in ways that make them want to stay generous, and even grow their giving.

This means that helping people have access to tools to use for online giving can make stewardship stronger in the on-site church by using the online church's tools. These two worlds are not in competition with each other – each offers access to a way of being church and following Jesus that can enhance the other. It is the ministry of Christ through the whole church that is enhanced.

Once you have a base from which you can help disciples of Jesus invest their resources in the work of Christ through the church, you can expand that doorway as a way of helping new people make commitments as well. In a world marked more by capitalism than by baptism, new people making a financial gift is close to an altar call for unchurched people. This kind of act usually requires some connection to the story, some support of the work or some touching of the heart before it happens. If someone gives to your ministry for the first time, notice it! Something is happening in that person's life that has connected their story to yours. This is about way more than money – this is about life.

For gifts like this to happen, three things are needed. First, the ministry has to touch the heart of a person – this can happen in person in a physical setting or online. In either case, the second thing that has to happen is that they feel moved to respond in some way and decide to give. The third thing that has to happen is that there has to be an accessible, easy way to give – not in a day or two, but right now!

This is where the financial world has changed significantly. It wasn't that long ago in the eyes of baby boomers and older people that everyone had a checkbook. ATM machines weren't around when they were growing up so you went to the bank to deposit and cash paychecks, take out cash for the week and pay some bills. Wallets were for carrying money. When you needed more money for your wallet or purse you wrote a check. Churches relied on a system of paper envelopes for people to insert weekly offerings (cash and/or checks) and then physically place them in an offering plate that was passed during worship. In many congregations, this is still where the majority of the resources come from; in some, it is still the only way.

As most of you reading this already know, the children of baby boomers, and especially their grandchildren, no longer function in this way (most baby boomers don't anymore either!). They use credit cards, debit cards, Google and Apple Pay, online banking and bill payments and may only touch cash once in a while. Many who have a "checking account" where money comes and goes couldn't find a paper check if their life depended on it. They look at statements online in real time and don't balance check registers. Somehow, to the amazement of the generations before them, it seems to work for many of them.

Previously effective methods of stewardship are being radically transformed by the online world, even for those ministries with no intentional online presence. For regular attenders, the use of online giving may function as a way of creating a pattern of generosity by using tools available through your web site, their bank or some other portal. The ability for newcomers to access these tools is important too.

Imagine you are a young person attending church in person for the first time in a long time, perhaps the first time ever. It is time for the offering and the ushers pass the offering plates and people put something to support the church in as it goes by. You open your wallet and you have a credit card, a debit card and a ten-dollar bill. Your phone uses Google Pay. What do you give? Well, to begin with, your only real option is to decide about the ten dollars. Give it and you are out of cash. Don't give it and you can only give nothing. You'd love to give a twenty, but there is no way to give that amount because you don't use checks – your debit card and cell phone apps are the doorways to your checking account. You drop in ten dollars out of guilt and feel a bit grumpy because it is all the cash you have and you'll need to restock at an ATM machine after church; you're also feeling guilty because you wanted to offer twenty. It is a lose-lose situation.

Suppose that same congregation had other giving tools in place – a variety of tools. To give you can text a code and an amount to a number on your phone and give what you want. Or you can go to the Google Play Store and get an app that allows you to set up a giving plan for supporting this ministry – one time today or ongoing. Or you can use your smartphone to go to the church's web site and click the donate button. Or they share PayPal info and you can go to PayPal and make a donation there – all during worship while the choir is singing a song and the ushers are passing the offering baskets. Or...?

Empowered by the tools, you are free to give what you want, make the commitment you desire and take a step that you feel good about. Congregations that only use traditional giving methods not only leave out options for giving, they leave out ways for people who want to connect to participate. Instead of feeling good about how this has turned out, our twenty-something visitor has left not doing what they wanted to do and not feeling good about the option they felt stuck with. Giving people multiple ways to respond empowers people. Not offering this not only impacts your giving – it impacts your ability to connect with new people in meaningful ways.

Making congregational changes

Sadly, even though everyone reading here may already know most of the things described in the paragraphs above, the majority of congregations have not implemented enough tools to deal with it. The leaders know it but have not changed to diversify the many ways, *especially for impromptu and situational giving,* that people can respond and invest their resources in the work of the church.

Every congregation should have online giving options – no exceptions. We are amazed at how resistant many congregations have been to this. Even after the pandemic, the percentage of congregations that still had no online giving options was significant. For many leaders, they simply don't want to pay to 2-3% transaction fees. As a result, they save a few hundred dollars in fees each year, while losing out on a few thousand dollars in giving each year. Remember, $97.00 that you get is still more than the $100 you don't get! Evidence is clear – online giving increases giving. This is not the place to be penny wise and pound foolish!

Enough on financial stewardship – the online world is transforming this. New giving tools and web apps are being developed all the time, some of them specifically for congregations. Keep up with the changes and use them! Don't let naysayers stop you in this area as every congregation can do this, no matter how big or how small. And every congregation will likely be strengthened by making progress in this.

Time and talents in an online world

Another stewardship conversation is about the use of time and talents in a hybrid church. Stewardship is about mobilizing the resources people have access to for use by God in whatever ways God can use them. Helping people become involved is something that happens in person in ways that are not always the same as online. Web tools allow for people to reflect and report what they have available in a more reflective way, perhaps at home. While many congregations have been using signup sheets, newsletters and in-person announcements to recruit people for ministry roles, adding online apps can completely transform how people get information about ministry opportunities as well as how they can respond.

There are increasing options for congregational apps that work on smartphones. These apps can be custom built for your congregation by providers who do this work as a specialization. There may also be options included in your online giving provider's services. Inside of a smartphone app can be a member directory, ministry information, messaging functions and a communication network that allows the congregation's leadership to communicate directly and instantly with every person who has the church app installed on their phone. A person's phone will notify them when they have a new message so they can check it immediately or when convenient. An app like this has incredible power to help with the stewardship of people and the use of their time and talents for ministry, and it facilitates quick response.

Suppose your congregation serves food for a local shelter every Tuesday. Tuesday morning a couple who are scheduled to volunteer get sick and they can't come. You are short two workers. In the old system, you were stuck scrambling to just let people know you needed someone. Even personal email might not be checked by most people until after work that evening or even a couple days later – too late to respond. But with a phone app, a message can be sent out to everyone saying that we need two people tonight. Cellphones are integral to daily life for many people and are checked routinely throughout the day. Two people respond to the issue and say they can help. By lunchtime, the issue of getting talents to the right place has been solved.

Being a hybrid congregation means using online tools to do both online and on-the-ground ministry and finding ways to be sure resources and gifts are available for use.

In addition, consider that the online world needs a new way of doing ministry. This means that online is not only a place to reach out and interact with people but also a place to mobilize people and their resources, time, gifts and skills. Your congregation being online can now invite people who are participating online to use their gifts and talents for the work of God through the church. Online stewardship may allow someone who's tangentially connected to the congregation to use their time and talents to advance the congregation's ministry, do something meaningful and become relationally connected to the faith community.

Remember, on-site ministry had clearer boundaries and more refined lines about who was in and out – often in tangible and subtle ways. Going online takes all these boundaries and blurs them (this can be very positive!). People may be participating online every week and leaders may not "see" them at all. Leadership will need to help people come out of the shadows and anonymity that online participation can provide by inviting people to be involved, asking questions that encourage people to interact with you and helping people move from a passive to a more engaged way of being a part of church life. It's not uncommon to begin asking questions about traditions, assumptions and rules about what membership means, what it requires, what defines active membership and who can be a member.

Stewardship and discipleship are closely related. Anything you can do as a leader to help people – on-site or online – to commit their lives to Christ and Christ's work and to mobilize their resources around that commitment is a powerful gift that the church can offer that helps give meaning and purpose to everyone's life. We have done this for centuries on-the-ground; now the online world is creating new ways for people to be challenged and encouraged to use their gifts for Christ's work both on-line and on-the-ground. The hybrid church is opening up new possibilities for an exciting and generous future!

For Reflection and Discussion

Scripture: Luke 19:1-10

(Jesus) entered and was passing through Jericho. There was a man named Zacchaeus. He was a chief tax collector, and he was rich. He was trying to see who Jesus was, and couldn't because of the crowd, because he was short. He ran on ahead, and climbed up into a sycamore tree to see him, for he was going to pass that way. When Jesus came to the place, he looked up and saw him, and said to him, "Zacchaeus, hurry and come down, for today I must stay at your house." He hurried, came down, and received him joyfully. When they saw it, they all murmured, saying, "He has gone in to lodge with a man who is a sinner."

Zacchaeus stood and said to the Lord, "Behold, Lord, half of my goods I give to the poor. If I have wrongfully exacted anything of anyone, I restore four times as much."

Jesus said to him, "Today, salvation has come to this house, because he also is a son of Abraham. For the Son of Man came to seek and to save that which was lost."

Questions

1. In the text, Zacchaeus meets Jesus and his life is changed in ways that make him unselfish and generous. What factors in your life have influenced you in ways that have increased your generosity? Who has inspired you?

2. What are your congregation's core values (both spoken and unspoken) regarding stewardship and generosity? Is it something that is talked about a lot or only once in a while or during an annual campaign?

3. Share the ways your congregation offers opportunities for online giving. Which are directed primarily toward members? Which allow for convenient situational giving by visitors or others who wish to make a one-time gift?

4. What is some aspect of stewardship which was discussed in this chapter which you think your congregation may underutilize and wish to learn more?

5. What is your stewardship strategy as hybrid congregation? What aspect of stewardship might you wish to expand in the near future? Who will be needed to make this change possible?

Prayer

God of abundance, you have formed us in your image and as you are generous and in Christ you have given us everything, even your own self. We see what a true generosity looks like in Christ and you call us to make giving central to our lives as well. Help each of us to be more generous in all aspects of our lives and help us lead the people in our ministry to be more generous and willing to invest in your work among us and through us, in Jesus name. Amen

9

Facilities in the Hybrid Church

One of the most interesting questions in a hybrid church is, "What about the building?" We saved this chapter for last, because the building is so fundamental to so many traditional congregations. How we begin to see the building may be the real test of whether a congregation fully makes the hybrid shift.

Carey Nieuwhof helps us to rethink our facilities when he says, "A lot of people use online to get people to come to the building. In the future, pastors will use the building to reach people online." (Engagement Online Summit, October 8, 2020) In other words, facility use will change and a small physical space (office, studio, etc.) will be well equipped and well utilized to reach and work with many people online.

What he means by this, is that buildings have been the focus in much of the last chapter of our ministry. We did outreach and invitations in order to get people to come to the building. Their arrival on site was a success. But now we have to rethink all of that. What we do from the building as a base for online ministry will now be focused on actually connecting with people *out there* who may never set foot inside. And that's OK!

In an on-the-ground ministry, the building is often the subject of a lot of time and energy (as well as money). Buildings have defined the church in many ways for the last century. When we "go to church" we mean that we are attending physically at a particular location. One of the first questions someone asks us when we say we attend church and share the name of our congregation is, "Where is that?"

There are often strong emotional ties to a building and facilities. When a congregation begins, one of the major benchmarks has historically been construction of the first building. Owning a "church" feels way more real to people than renting space in "someone else's church" or leasing a storefront location. Experience consulting shows that, "whose building will we keep?" is one of the major barriers to two or more congregations merging and forming a new, more effective ministry. In fact, thousands of congregations have opted for stripped down ministry and almost no staffing in order to keep their buildings and property. There is a lot of emotional investment and energy in our facilities!

Online ministry presents almost the opposite mindset. Rather than concerns about physical space, the questions become, "What kind of online tools will we use?" and "What kind of bandwidth do we need in order to use them without issues?" Online ministry can be done from a rented space, a leader's basement or home office, and even from a coffee shop with a good Wi-Fi connection. There are some successful online ministries where almost all the work is done from a smartphone that fits in someone's pocket and is formatted in ways that allow participants to be fully involved with just a smartphone of their own. So physical space is almost a non-concern for some leaders working online.

So, what is a hybrid church to do with these two competing mindsets – one where a physical building is central to the ministry's identity and another where having a physical building is not a fundamental element?

Remember that being a hybrid church takes both realities seriously. There will be ministry that is online and doesn't have a need for a sizeable physical footprint. And there will also be ministry where people are physically present and where the facilities matter. You may be in a setting where your building remains a very important part of your work. If you are doing online ministry based there you will need to decide what tools to use and be sure that you have the bandwidth you need to use them seamlessly throughout your ministry.

Technology Matters

As we begin to think about the physical needs for a hybrid ministry, online capacity may be one of the main issues that presents a challenge. For example, in my (Dave's) own congregation we had a contract with our cable provider for internet coverage that was more than adequate for our office needs. Emails came and went with no issues; browsing online was efficient. If someone was checking out a streaming video for a class or Facebook post, the videos buffered effectively, and no one was hindered or slowed down as our staff worked. More than one person could operate at the same time and no one's work was impaired by too many people fighting for bandwidth.

But when we went online for streaming our worship service, suddenly issues arose. The Wi-Fi extender that we had to bring a signal into the sanctuary had been adequate for showing a video during worship but proved too slow for live streaming worship out to the world. When we looked into this more fully, we discovered that internet speeds in the sanctuary were only half of what they were in the offices – the Wi-Fi extender's ability to relay the signal still resulted in a loss of functional speed. When we looked at our internet provider contract, we discovered that we had not upgraded our bandwidth since the contract began nine years earlier and what had been a good internet speed then was now barely adequate for the online needs and capacities that had become possible during that time. Even though our usage had not presented any major issues, taking the ministry online caused us to hit a wall. We immediately upgraded our contract and increased our download and upload speeds by a factor of ten.

However, even upgrading did not result in a perfect outcome. Our extender had maximum speed limitations that it could handle as it repeated the signal, so our sanctuary speeds were still less that we wanted to have. To do what needed to be done, we ran a physical ethernet cable from the offices where the main signal came into our building and where the main router was located. Hardwiring the sanctuary required getting a new, up-to-date, higher speed wireless router for the sanctuary in order to give the sanctuary the full benefit of our increased capacity. It eventually involved hardwiring our worship broadcasting equipment and discontinuing the use of Wi-Fi to upload livestreaming. We then redid the office based on the sanctuary receiving our core Wi-Fi capacity and had to redo our wireless printer network to match the new configuration. I could share more but you get the idea!

All of this is to say that to be a physically landed church with a serious online presence will require you to do what you can to make the physical facilities have a dependable and efficient online capacity. Look at the bandwidth that is available to you at your address. In many urban areas you can get enough to run multiple online ministries at the same time! In some rural areas you may still be struggling to get enough bandwidth to do much more than basic email and web browsing. What you can get in your location will be the first line of determining what you can do to make your building hybrid functional.

Also, be sure that the places in your building that are

most central to online ministry have the highest priority for actually getting use of that capacity. Most facilities have their office space as the technology center. Depending what your online ministry looks like, giving priority to the sanctuary, a conference room or other spaces may require rethinking your entire network, running physical cables to increase access and reliability, and making major shifts and upgrades to things you have been satisfied with for a long time. There will be at least some cost to acquiring and installing the physical things you need implement this (routers, ethernet cables, etc.) and perhaps an increase in monthly costs due to higher monthly bills from your provider for improved services.

Rethinking space

If your current facility is in a location that cannot be fitted with what is needed to be a hybrid congregation and you are committed to doing both on-the-ground and online ministry well, there are other alternatives available to you. For example, many rural congregations are out in the country and have few options for getting high grade internet service, but many of these same country churches may be less than ten miles from a neighboring town on a busy highway with much better options. Perhaps online ministry is something that is done in partnership with a neighboring congregation using their location and sharing the work and costs. Or perhaps an office in that village can be rented affordably and the physical ministry is done at the country building and the online ministry is based in the village office space. It may be that moving the office staff into the rented office in town also gives the church a chance for a new physical presence throughout the week in a more populated location and from which it can be more physically present to an audience on-the-ground as well. Getting better online tools may improve office capacity in other ways and provide benefits to the on-the-ground ministry as well as access to a meaningful online ministry. Don't let a roadblock or initial costs stop you from thinking imaginatively about other options. It may be that a solution that is more challenging to discern is also more fruitful and creative in the long run.

Another important consideration is to remember that being a strong online ministry in a hybrid church isn't really just about livestreaming worship from the sanctuary. This may be a core function, but many effective online ministries don't even have a sanctuary and are still able to have online worship. Leadership leads from some other places and streams sermons, lessons, prayers, music and more. It may be recorded ahead and edited, much like most TV programs. It may be livestreamed as it is led, but never from a physical sanctuary.

This is an important truth to reckon with. Your space and your audience may prompt very different choices for each ministry site as you do this work. In addition, as we (Dave's congregation) looked at our online worship and also scanned the web for other good examples, we recognized that our sanctuary looked cluttered and wasn't ideal for an online presence. We had to make changes in the sanctuary to make it work for online. The other alternative – equally valid – would have been to stream online worship from some place other than the sanctuary.

A Changing "Place" for Ministry

So how do we rethink or redesign facilities to do ministry in areas that have historically been delivered only through someone being physically present? How can we have people in the building and out of the building interacting in one ministry activity at the same time?

Whatever physical location(s) a congregation chooses as the base for implementing hybrid ministry can also be equipped with the capacity to handle physical ministry that interacts with online people at the same time. This presents additional concerns and probably additional setup costs but can radically change how education opportunities and leadership meetings happen going forward.

In the best of all worlds, a congregation will benefit from having at least one meeting/conference/classroom which is spacious enough to accommodate a good-sized meeting or class and also has capacity for online participation during the same event. This will allow people to come to the building and be physically present with each other while other people stream into the same meeting or class remotely using online tools like Skype, Zoom or similar streaming platforms.

A well-equipped room will have at least the following things:

1. Strong and consistent internet access so that as classes and meetings are streamed the buffering time doesn't result in a choppy experience for those participating online.

2. Good technology for people accessing the event from either platform to see, hear and interact effectively with people across platforms. This means a good web camera, an adequately large TV/monitor, a good speaker system and quality microphone(s)

for people in the physical meeting space.

Doing this well also means good communication with all who are participating so that they understand that if the congregation's technology is up to speed then participants will be responsible for whatever needs to happen on their end "out there" somewhere. The phone, tablet or laptop they are using as well as the access to internet that they have will impact each person's experience, even if the group's overall experience is set up perfectly at the church facility.

Many of you reading this have probably been on an online class or meeting where someone's voice or picture becomes choppy or even inaudible, not through the overarching technology issues where you are but because that person has something going on where they are. This can be distracting for everyone involved, even though the issue only directly impacts one participant. So, it is important to manage expectations, help people diagnose what is and isn't working, and be gracious with each other – especially so when things are being rolled out and unexpected issues arise on the fly.

To do this work effectively, congregational leaders will determine which room(s) will best accommodate this. There are concerns related to technology to be taken into account (can we get good online bandwidth to that space?) and concerns related to implementation (can we configure or reconfigure the layout of the room to provide people who are both online and physically present to have a positive and effective experience?).

Don't underestimate the emotional nature of these decisions. Remember how devoted people can be to physical spaces familiar surroundings in the church. It may be that the best space for signal access and reconfiguring a room has been a favorite space for something else. Taking a room that is already used for this kind of on-the-ground work could easily become the best space to use for online and hybrid ministry (that's good). But the need new for furniture and for the room's physical space to be reoriented to accommodate a monitor, web camera and conference microphones for this new use may prove to be a source of stress and resistance. Think through ahead of time how a decision to upgrade some things that seems obvious or needed to most people may affect others. Remodeling, getting rid of beloved furniture donated by a member or moving things around can stir up emotions, stress and uncertainty for some people. So be sure to keep your mission in the foreground, communicate well, listen for grief, respond to concerns and process things well – all while still moving forward in meaningful ways.

Keep in mind that on-the-ground ministries may have been effective in part due to their commitment outside groups and community use. You may be accustomed to having a Tuesday evening Bible study in a classroom while a Twelve Step Group is meeting in the fellowship hall. Many community groups are also exploring hybrid access to meetings as well and some want or need both a physical meeting space and the ability for others to stream in. Planning for additional rooms equipped with both meeting space and technology access will help anticipate the needs of having more than one group meeting at same time. Or, if more than one space is not possible, speak with community partners to find the best schedule to maximize ministry and accommodate each other's needs.

Lastly, remember that being a hybrid church brings with it all sorts of unforeseen collateral impacts. You may discover that going online is attractive to more people than being on-site. You may find you have more classrooms than you need, even though you are offering educational opportunities to more people than ever before. If so, does the addition of extra educational space create the opportunity for adding an online staff person and giving them an office where there wasn't office space before? Or do community partners need affordable or free office space and now you can provide a new gift to the community?

You may find that your physical worship attendance drops by twenty-five percent and is fifty people less each week on-site while your online worship attendance adds three hundred people and your overall reach more than doubles. This doesn't mean you won't still need a sanctuary, but you may go from three on-site services to two, drop a weekend service that has been on-site and offer an online midweek service instead, or choose to have one larger physical service and one online service. Going online may change your on-site offerings dramatically. If you have a parking issue, online ministry may solve it and that much needed purchase of the lot next door that you have had your eye on for several years may now be unnecessary. The number of seats in your sanctuary may not match the new reality and you may end up rearranging them to make seating and capacity match.

For the hybrid congregation, facility management will present new options and challenges. But the possibilities and creativity are only limited by the openness of your hearts and the size of your imagination.

For Reflection and Discussion

Scripture: John 2:13-17

The Passover of the Jews was at hand, and Jesus went up to Jerusalem. He found in the temple those who sold oxen, sheep, and doves, and the changers of money sitting. He made a whip of cords, and threw all out of the temple, both the sheep and the oxen; and he poured out the changers' money and overthrew their tables. To those who sold the doves, he said, "Take these things out of here! Don't make my Father's house a marketplace!" His disciples remembered that it was written, "Zeal for your house will eat me up."

Questions

1. Jesus had a desire that the building that was central to his faith not be misused to meet the desires of sinful people – but used to honor God. If a facility is not primarily about us, but about what God wants, how do you think you should view the facility your congregation currently uses? Is this the way most people think of it or would there be disagreement or tension over your answer?

2. What is your experience of your congregation's building? In what ways do you personally use it in a typical week?

3. How much of your building is used throughout the week? How often and by who? Have you talked to them about their needs and how technology access would make their work easier or better?

4. In which ways does your building enhance or hinder your ministry? What can you do with it or to it to enhance its shortcomings?

5. When you think of creating hybrid space in your facility, which rooms or spaces make the most sense? What is needed to make that happen?

Prayer

God of Spirit and truth, we know that for you the physical world is not a limiting thing, but an expression of your infinite reach and love. Yet we are bound by this world and sometimes our imaginations are limited by that as well. Help us to re-envision how our facilities can be used to do ministry in the everchanging world in which we live. Help us to see them as gifts from our past as well as tools for our future. Give us the imagination, the courage and the resources to work with the needs of the people of our congregation and the needs of our community as we rethink and retool. Keep us mindful of the many people who are online but who may never set foot in our building and find ways to reach out to them. In Jesus' name we pray. Amen

Conclusion

As we come to the end of this book, we know that this is most likely still early in your journey. If you are reading a book like this, you are probably curious about how to move forward into the future from the on-the-ground ministry that is familiar to you, while venturing out into the online world to do ministry in ways that are new.

That means that you will do well to live in a tension – the tension between being assertive and driven balanced with the need to make space to fail and be gracious (with yourself and others).

If you don't work hard at this, really hard, it will not happen. This is a big leap and not everyone will make it. In fact, only those who work hard at it probably have a real shot at doing it well.

But it is also important to remember that making big adaptive changes and implementing the technical things to make it happen will require learning, thinking, processing, and trial and error. You are going to make mistakes and so will the people you work with. If you aren't gracious with each other, the drive to find the new church may destroy something else that is important – your souls.

So, balance hard work with real grace. Leave out either of these and you will be assured of a mess. Include both, and whatever comes of it will become what it will become.

Also remember that a book like this is to be a catalyst to thought and action. In the pages of this book are thoughts and ideas and examples to help you work through a variety of areas of ministry. You don't need to implement all of them at once – or even all of them in total. Pray, discuss and reflect with the people in your context. Watch and learn from others who are working in the areas of ministry that make sense for you to do in hybrid ways.

As you do this, remember, while technical changes are about using skills, adaptive changes require wisdom – the wisdom to know what to do and where to do it is a key to all of this.

You probably also noticed various places in the previous chapters where staff references were made. To go online in new ways means that staff roles have to change. Some of this may be relatively simple – staff do what they do in ways they always have. But some of this may be really hard – staff will have to change how they spend their time or have to do work they have no training in. Some key functions related to technology and online media may mean bringing on new staff and retraining and repurposing volunteers. New roles will arise. Some favorite roles may change or even disappear.

This can be hard to do. In some cases, not everyone can simply take up (or wants) a new job description. That means there can be real stress as the ministry moves to new ways of doing things in the new online world. Be loving as you do this. Grace and compassion are marks of Christ in us. But don't let the difficulty of these conversations prevent you from having them. No ministry will function in an area where its staff, no matter how small, aren't able to give leadership and/or support to it.

We know that almost everyone reading this book was introduced to online ministry in significant ways as a result of the COVID pandemic. The quick move from not being online to Easter worship online was fueled by a mix of real need and adrenaline. In that sense, the beginning of the journey was somewhat instinctive.

But we also know that almost none of us are near the end of the journey to fully being online – we all have a lot to learn. The online world is changing so fast that even keeping up is hard – much less making real progress.

That means we are all somewhere in the middle. The middle part of a long journey is often the hardest. The rush of getting started wears off and the adrenaline levels drop. But the finish line (if such a thing exists in the world of church change) is still far off and mostly out of sight. It will take persistent effort to keep going. All of us will need help from others. Find partners in the work. Look for a coach or consultant(s) who can help you with charting a course, getting new skills and sticking with the work. Remind yourself often of why you do this work and why God cares about the online world so much (hint: it's because almost EVERYONE is out there!).

We are reminded of "kintsugi," the Japanese art made by taking broken pottery and reassembling it using gold to repair the seams. For a while, the church may look like it is simply broken into a lot of places. Big changes reveal weak places quickly! But the ongoing work will not discard what we have been or from where we have come. It will use them to reshape a new church for a new time – one that may be more beautiful than we can imagine.

So, we end with encouragement. God can and will take what we have been in Christ. Some of it may die – that's always the case. But the God we meet in Jesus is a God of resurrection and new life. We don't often think of this, but all of us grew up in a post-pandemic church. In fact, the most recent one is just one of many, many plagues and pandemics throughout the centuries. In every case, the world has been changed and new protocols put in place. For those born after it was over, they were just "normal." No one told us what it was like before.

Remember, God has remained committed to the church in every new era as history has moved forward. This was not God's first pandemic and we are not inventing the first post-pandemic church – just the most recent one. And because the church is ultimately not the church because of human effort but rather it is a work of God – whatever comes of this, the reign of God still lies boldly on the horizon.